CL 1107699 2

D0525710

ESSENTIAL
ICELAND

Original by Ann F Stonehouse
Updated by Ann F Stonehouse

© AA Media Limited 2009
First published 2007
Revised 2009

Series Editor Karen Kemp
Series Designer Sharon Rudd
Cartographic Editor Anna Thompson

ISBN: 978-0-7495-6126-0

Published by AA Publishing, a trading name of AA Media Limited, whose registered office is Fanum House, Basing View, Basingstoke, Hampshire RG21 4EA. Registered number 06112600.

Colour separation: MRM Graphics Ltd
Printed and bound in Italy by Printer Trento S.r.l.

A03804
Maps in this title produced from mapping © MAIRDUMONT / Falk Verlag 2009

About this book

The essence of Iceland pages 6–17
Introduction; Features; Food and drink; Short break including the 10 Essentials

Planning pages 18–31
Before you go; Getting there; Getting around; Being there

Best places to see pages 32–53
The highlights of any visit to Iceland

Best things to do pages 54–67
Good places to have lunch; top activities; Reykjavík nightlife and more

Exploring pages 68–155
The best places to visit in Iceland, organized by area

Maps
All map references are to the maps on the covers. For example, Reykjavík has the reference 🕂 18K – indicating the grid square in which it is to be found.

Admission prices
Inexpensive: under ISK500
Moderate: ISK500–ISK900
Expensive: over ISK900

Hotel prices
Prices are per room per night:
£ budget (under ISK7,000);
££ moderate (ISK7,000–12,000);
£££ expensive to luxury (over ISK12,000)

Restaurant prices
Two-course meal per person without drinks:
£ budget (under ISK1,500);
££ moderate (ISK1,500–2,200);
£££ expensive (over ISK2,200)

Icelandic characters
In this book we have shown the Icelandic character ð as Ð/ð , pronounced as a hard 'th' as in 'then'. The Icelandic character Þ/þ, is pronounced as a soft 'th' as in 'thistle' (see also page 30).

Contents

BEST THINGS TO DO

54 – 67

EXPLORING...

68 – 155

The essence of...

First-time visitors arriving at Keflavík airport look out on the surprisingly fresh-looking lunar landscape of Iceland and wonder what they've done. Most find themselves hooked and come back again and again.

features

At a mere 20 million years old, this is the youngest country in Europe, an island just bigger than Ireland (350km/217 miles from south to north, 540km/335 miles from west to east) and lying across the vast undersea split known as the Mid-Atlantic Ridge, where two of the great plates of the earth's surface are pulling apart. This makes Iceland one of the world's most volcanically active sites, but it offers much more than just a live geography lesson.

For a start, it's a great place for outdoor activities, including hiking, horse-riding, fishing and adventure sports. It's also an important breeding place for many rare birds and is blessed with sparkling clean air, the 'midnight sun', endless summer days and mid-winter Northern Lights. The mountains, fjords, rivers and waterfalls provide sweeping landscapes and diverse flora.

The Icelanders themselves generally welcome visitors and are proud to show off their country. Despite a small population of around 300,000, Icelanders read more books per capita than any other country, love the latest gadgets and fashions, and usually speak several languages, including English. A vibrant and unique music scene has emerged here, with bands such as Sigur Rós and Björk known worldwide. Icelanders worked hard to achieve one of the highest standards of living in the world, however, at the end of 2008 the country's economic bubble burst, with considerable casualties, including its major banks.

Facilities for visitors have improved in recent years, but costs are high as so much has to be imported. The changeable weather and many unmade roads are notorious, but they needn't stop you getting to most places, though the remote and rocky interior is only accessible in high summer.

Make sure you don't try to see everything in one visit – the ring road looks a temptingly short way to get around, but if you don't stop and explore properly, you'll have missed most of what Iceland really has to offer. And the rewards are fantastic.

ICELAND'S FAMOUS
LEIFUR EIRÍKSSON (FL. AD1000)
Eldest son of Icelandic Viking Erik the Red, 'Leif the Lucky' is widely credited with the earliest European discovery of North America. He set sail from Greenland around AD1000 and is believed to have made landings on Baffin Island and down the east coast to the tip of Newfoundland before returning safely with claims of a lush land of paradise.

SNORRI STURLUSON (1179–1241)
Snorri was a powerful chief, Lawspeaker at the Alþing (parliament) and descendant of the Viking hero and skaldic poet Egill Skallagrímson. He wrote the great Icelandic *Prose Edda* (a recording of Norse mythology), *Heimskringla* (the history of Norwegian kings) and probably *Egil's Saga* as well.

HALLDÓR LAXNESS (1902–98)
Born in Reykjavík, Halldór Laxness had his first novel, *Child of Nature*, published when he was just 17. He went on to write prolifically and was awarded the Nobel Prize for Literature in 1955. His best-known novel is *Independent People* (1946), set in the early 20th century, giving a realistically grim insight into peasant farming in Iceland.

BJÖRK GUDMUNDSDÓTTIR (1965–)
Björk cut her first disc at the age of 11 and became a member of punk-funk band The Sugarcubes, hitting world stardom with their song *Birthday* in 1988. She's since become Iceland's most popular export in her own recording right, with an inimitable vocal style and a constant ability to shock.

food & drink

Of necessity Icelanders live around the coastline of their island and, since fishing supports some 70 per cent of the economy, it's not really surprising that fish features largely in their diet.

Haddock *(ýsa)* is the national favourite, fresh and boiled or fried lightly. Cod *(thorskur)* is largely exported, but you may find delicacies such as cod chins on the menu – try them, they are rich and delicious. Catfish *(steinbítur)* and halibut *(lúða)* are also widely available, and pickled herring *(síld)* is often served at breakfast. You'll see fish drying on wooden racks along the coast; this used to be a staple food to see poor farmers through the winter, but now it's something of a delicacy. Called *harðfiskur*, it looks like shredded loofah and has a mild, not unpleasant fish taste, eaten smeared with butter *(smjör)*. Try it at the market in Kolaportið (➤ 78–79) before you buy. Pickling fish in whey is a speciality, celebrated in the Þorrablót festival in January/February (➤ 22).

Shellfish is also excellent, notably the small lobster *(humar)*. For freshwater fish, try the salmon *(lax)*, trout *(silungur)* and Arctic char *(bleikja)*.

The most notorious Icelandic dish is carefully rotted shark flesh *(hákarl)*, which, when swilled down with a shot of the spirit *brennivín*, is supposed to induce a rapid state of intoxication – try it if you dare.

Icelanders boast that their lamb, fed on good pasture, comes ready-seasoned, and it's certainly very good. Roasted, it's a traditional Sunday lunch, but you'll also find it salted *(saltkjöt)* and, particularly around Christmas, smoked like ham *(hangikjöt)*. Singed sheep head is a less appealing traditional item, eaten hot or cold, and you can buy it ready-pressed and gelled *(sviðasulta)*.

If you are determined to try the unusual, some restaurants serve puffin, guillemot and even fulmar, and at certain times you'll also see their mottled eggs for sale. The Icelanders have been eating them for years without denting the population, so don't feel too bad about it.

A ready supply of fruit and vegetables came late to this remote island, but the wonders of geothermal power harnessed to greenhouses in centres such as Hveragerði (► 101) mean that much more is now available, if not cheap. Bananas are actually grown in Akureyri.

Small cinnamon biscuits *(kex)* can be bought by the bagfull in any supermarket – and look out for the tasty doughnut knot, *kleinur*. A sweet, dark rye-bread is cooked slowly in the hot lava *(rúgbrauð)*, and at Christmas fragile flat cakes of thinly rolled and cut pastry are deep-fried *(laufabrauð* – see them out of season in the Christmas shop at Akureyri). Rye pancakes *(flatbrauð)* and large sweet pancakes are also eaten.

The low-fat dairy product *skyr* is widely available. Somewhere between cream cheese and yogurt, it is good served with cream and sugar or fresh fruit, and it also makes an excellent basis for cheesecake. Milk labelling can be confusing — *nýmjólk* is the normal stuff, while *léttmjólk* is semi-skimmed, *undanrenna* is skimmed and *súrmjólk* is like thin yogurt. And of course ice cream *(ís)* is eaten everywhere.

short break

Everything about Iceland is fascinating but there are certain experiences which should not be missed. If you only have a short time to visit Iceland, here are some of the essentials:

● **Relax in a thermally heated 'hot-pot';** they don't come more comfortable than the Blue Lagoon (➤ 34–35), but local swimming pools have them too.

● **Take the lift** to the top of the Hallgrímskirkja tower for the best views over Reykjavík (➤ 40–41).

● **Visit a Reykjavík sculpture gallery** and get to know more about Icelandic art – there's public sculpture everywhere and it's more fun if you know what you're looking at.

● **Go for a ride** on an Icelandic horse and try the unique 'fifth gait' for yourself (➤ 59) – it's a leisurely way to explore the countryside.

- **Treat yourself to a trip onto a glacier** by snow-scooter or snow-tractor. Vatnajökull is the biggest in Europe but there are plenty of other choices.

- **Get off the Hringvegur (ring road)** into the mountains and the interior – and if the bumpy state of the side roads puts you off, enjoy the advantages of an organized tour.
- **Watch puffins,** everybody's favourite seabird.
- **Eat fish** – there's a great selection of top restaurants to choose from. Try Við Tjörnina in Reykjavík (➤ 115), or Bautinn in Akureyri (➤ 140) for the best.

- **Talk to the locals** for real insights – Icelanders have a keen national identity and pride, and are usually pleased to tell you more about their country.
- **Explore a steaming geothermal area** to understand why Iceland is as it is.

Planning

Before you go

WHEN TO GO

JAN	FEB	MAR	APR	MAY	JUN	JUL	AUG	SEP	OCT	NOV	DEC
0.5°C	-1°C	-1.4°C	4°C	6.6°C	10.1°C	11.1°C	11.3°C	8.3°C	2.9°C	2.2°C	1.2°C
33°F	30°F	29°F	39°F	44°F	50°F	52°F	52.3°F	47°F	37°F	36°F	34°F

High season ▢ Low season

Roads across the remote volcanic interior are only open to vehicles in July and August. At this time the rest of Iceland is green and relatively balmy, with almost 24-hour daylight, but it can be windy and wet. The main tourist season extends through June and September. In winter or spring, be prepared for shorter, grey days and driving snow, which can block minor roads and make routes hazardous – ask for snow tyres on your hire car, and check road conditions ahead. Few attractions outside the capital are open in winter. The Northern Lights may be seen under still, clear conditions in autumn, and between November and February. In the north of the island, the sun does not fully set in June; correspondingly, in January there may be only 3.5 hours of daylight in that region.

WHAT YOU NEED

		UK	Germany	USA	Netherlands	Spain
● Required	Some countries require a passport to remain valid for a minimum period (usually at least six months) beyond the date of entry – contact their consulate or embassy or your travel agent for details.					
○ Suggested						
▲ Not required						
Passport (or National Identity Card where applicable)		●	○	●	○	○
Visa (regulations can change – check before you travel)		▲	▲	▲	▲	▲
Onward or Return Ticket		▲	▲	▲	▲	▲
Health Inoculations (tetanus and polio)		▲	▲	▲	▲	▲
Health Documentation (➤ 21, Health Insurance)		▲	▲	▲	▲	▲
Travel Insurance		●	●	●	●	●
Driving Licence (national)		●	●	●	●	●
Car Insurance Certificate		○	○	●	○	○
Car Registration Document		●	●	●	●	●

WEBSITES

www.icetourist.is
Official website packed with information on everything from culture to landscape

www.vegagerdin.is/english
The Icelandic Road Administration's site with essential information if you are travelling out of season

TOURIST OFFICES AT HOME

In the UK: Iceland Air, 172 Tottenham Court Road, 3rd floor, London W1T 7LY ☎ 020 7874 1000; www.visiticeland.com

In the USA: Icelandic Tourist Board 655 Third Avenue, New York, NY 10017 ☎ 212/885-9700; www.icelandtouristboard.com

In Germany: Iceländisches Fremdenverkehrsamt, City Centre, Frankfurterstrasse, 181, D-63263 Neu-Isenburg, Germany ☎ 6102 254484; www.icetourist.de

HEALTH INSURANCE

Visitors from the EU are entitled to reciprocal state medical care and should take an EHIC (European Health Insurance Card), which covers basic treatment. Citizens from elsewhere will need medical insurance. Note that extra medical insurance will not necessarily cover you for all activities. There is a 24-hour emergency ward at the National Hospital, Fossvogur (tel: 543 2000), and 24-hour duty doctors may be contacted (tel: 5251000). For 24-hour medical information tel: 1770.

Ask at your hotel or guest house for details of local English-speaking dentists. For emergency dental cover in Reykjavík tel: 575 0505.

TIME DIFFERENCES

GMT	Iceland	→ Germany	← USA (NY)	→ Netherlands	→ Spain
12 noon	12 noon	1PM	7AM	1PM	1PM

Iceland is on GMT all year. It does not go on to daylight saving time.

NATIONAL HOLIDAYS

1 Jan *New Year's Day*	Jun *Whit Sunday*	26 Dec *Boxing Day*
Apr *Maundy Thursday,*	Jun *Whit Monday*	31 Dec *New Year's Eve*
Good Friday, Easter	17 Jun *National Day*	
Sunday, Easter Monday	Aug *Bank Holiday*	Most shops, offices and
Apr *First Day of Summer*	*Monday*	museums close on these
1 May *Labour Day*	24 Dec *Christmas Eve*	days.
May *Ascension Day*	25 Dec *Christmas Day*	

WHAT'S ON WHEN

1 January *New Year:* Celebrations start the afternoon before – a great excuse for bonfires and fireworks.

6 January *Twelfth Night:* More bonfires and fireworks to brighten up the long dark nights.

Late January–late February *Þorrablót:* Celebration of traditional winter foods. Delicacies such as whey-pickled fish and rams' testicles are washed down with *brennivín* – a type of schnapps.

April *Shrove Tuesday:* 'Bursting Day' *(Sprengidalur)* is commemorated by feasting on lamb and pea soup. The previous Monday is 'Bun Day' *(Bolludagur)*, when children go round threatening to beat the grown-ups with sticks, and demanding buns.

Easter: Everything closes from Maundy Thursday to Easter Monday. On Ash Wednesday *(Öskudagur)*, children attempt to hang little bags of ashes on the backs of unsuspecting adults.

Around 20 April *First Day of Summer (Sumardagurinn fyrsti):* An important landmark Thursday which is celebrated in laid-back carnival style.

Early June *Seamen's Day (Sjómannadagurinn):* Harbours are filled with ships and vessels of all sizes on this Sunday, and celebrations include rowing races and tugs of war.

17 June *National Day (Þjóðhátíð):* Carnival-type festivities are held all over Iceland.

Late June *The Arctic Open:* This cheerful four-day golf championship, open to professionals and amateurs, is played through the light summer nights on the world's most northerly golf course. At Akureyri, it lies 65° 40' north of the Equator.

International Viking Festival: Now an annual fixture, this is an unmissable

Viking jamboree of singing, dancing, eating and fighting in the best traditions, held at the Viking Village in Hafnarfjörður.

Early July *Höfn Lobster Festival (Hátíð á Höfn):* A big party with music, dance, competitions and feasting.

First weekend in August *Herring Festival (Síldarævintri):* Extensive celebrations in Siglufjorður, former herring capital of Iceland.

Early August *Westmann Islands Festival (Þjóðhátíð):* Independence Day party, held on Heimaey, with barbecues, bonfires and roistering.

September *Reltir:* Round-ups on horse-back are held all over the country, bringing sheep and horses down from the hills before winter sets in.

23 December *Þorláksmessa:* Celebrated in the best restaurants by the eating of cured skate.

24–25 December *Christmas* officially starts at noon on the 24th, and presents are exchanged on that day.

Yuletide Lads

Christmas for children in Iceland has its own special dimension. According to tradition, 13 boisterous 'Yuletide lads' come to call, one each night leading up to 25 December, to leave a small gift in the child's shoe placed in a window for that purpose. (If the child has been naughty, there'll be a potato in there in the morning instead.) The lads are pranksters and nicknamed accordingly – 'Sausage Snatcher', 'Door Slammer', 'Candle Snuffer' and so on. They are ruled over by a fearsome matriarch called Gryla, who eats bad children for breakfast. Her cat eats anyone without new clothes to wear on Christmas Day.

Getting there

ARRIVING
Iceland Express (www.icelandexpress.com) is a budget airline that connects daily with London, Alicante, Barcelona, Berlin and Copenhagen, with more destinations in summer. Icelandair (www.icelandair.net) is the chief operator of international flights, flying from London, Glasgow, Manchester, Copenhagen, Oslo, Paris, Stockholm, Amsterdam, Frankfurt, Boston, Minneapolis, New York, Orlando and others in summer. SAS flies from Oslo. A regular shuttle bus operates between Keflavík airport and Reykjavík. Flybus transport into the centre of Reykjavík leaves after every incoming flight, cost ISK1,250 (tel: 562 1011; www.flybus.is).

FERRIES
The weekly car ferry from Denmark to Seyðisfjörður calls at Shetland, the Faroes and Norway. Contact Smyril Line, Yviri við Strond 1, PO Box 370, FO-110, Tórshavn, Faroes (tel: +298 345900; www.smyril-line.is).

CUSTOMS
YES Goods obtained duty-free. Limits:1L of spirits (up to 47% alcohol); 1L of wine (up to 21% alcohol) or 6L of beer; or 3L of wine and 200 cigarettes or 250g of other tobacco products. You must be over 20 to benefit from alcohol allowances, and over 18 for the tobacco allowances.

   Horse-riding clothing and angling gear that has been used outside Iceland, including gloves and boots, requires a certificate of disinfection according to the regulations. Visitors are allowed to bring food into the country duty-free, for their own use in Iceland.

NO Uncooked vegetables, eggs, meat or dairy products; narcotics; firearms; unlicensed plants or animals.

Getting around

DRIVING

- Drive on the right.
- Speed limit on main tarmac roads: 90kph (56mph)
  Speed limit on main gravel roads: 80kph (50mph)
  Speed limit in populated areas: 30/50kph (19/31mph)
- Seatbelts are mandatory in front and rear seats.
- Icelandic law forbids driving after drinking alcohol, and the penalties are severe.
- Unleaded petrol is available as 95 octane (regular) and 98 octane (super). Filling stations around Reykjavík are open daily 7:30am–8pm or later; around the country, times may vary, and some are open only in summer. Some filling stations have automats which take ISK500, ISK1,000 and ISK2,000 notes and credit and debit cards after hours, but these do not always work. Petrol stations can be few and far between, so don't let your fuel run low.
- In case of breakdown, telephone your car rental company for emergency assistance.

CAR RENTAL

Car rental is expensive so shop around for the best deal – you may be able to combine with a fly-drive or farm-stay package, for example. A 4WD is essential if you plan going far off the main roads, and spiked snow tyres for winter driving in snowy conditions. Check the cover – rental companies may not insure you on some routes.

MOTORING INFORMATION

Driving conditions Route 1 is now tarmac, but other roads across the country are often unsurfaced gravel. Be prepared to slow right down when passing other vehicles, as loose gravel can be thrown up and road edges are soft; be cautious at narrow bridges and blind summits, and be prepared to give way (flashing headlights usually mean 'I'm coming through'). Stay on the roads and tracks. The natural environment is fragile and off-road driving carries heavy fines.

Headlights must be switched on at all times when driving, day and night. On roundabouts, cars on the inside lane have right of way.

Driving in the interior Many roads across central Iceland are open for only a few weeks in high summer, as weather conditions can change very quickly. If you're planning a trip, consult tourist information and locals before you set out and be especially cautious at unbridged rivers.

Animals Note that sheep, horses and cattle may stray onto the roads and you are liable to pay compensation for any animal injured or killed. Farm dogs chasing cars can be a particular hazard.

On the road On your travels you may find that, with such a small and scattered resident population, there are long distances between towns with restaurants. The network of petrol stations comes to the rescue here, acting not only as essential toilet stops, but always with a pot of hot coffee on tap and usually offering a range of other snacks, including the ubiquitous hotdogs. And among the household-name chocolate bars, you'll discover liquorice in every conceivable form – very much a local favourite.

PUBLIC TRANSPORT

Internal flights Flugfélag Íslands (Air Iceland, tel: 570 3030; www.airiceland.net) is the main operator of domestic flights and flights to the Faroes and Greenland, out of Reykjavík. Mýflug (tel: 464 4400; www.myflug.is) operates sightseeing flights from Mývatn. Flugfélag Vestmannæyja has regular flights to the Westmann Islands (tel: 481 3255).

Buses Reykjavík's main BSÍ coach terminal is at Vatnsmýrarvegur 10 (tel: 562 1011). There are regular daily coach services around the country, even in winter. You can buy good value 'passport' tickets if you

intend to travel widely on the network. The complete bus timetable is available at www.nat.is.

Ferries Local ferries operate between the mainland and islands or remote areas. There are more frequent services in summer.

Viðey ☎ 533 5055
Flatey ☎ 438 1450
Hrísey ☎ 695 5544/458 8900
Westmann Islands ☎ 481 2800

Urban transport Reykjavík's yellow city buses operate from Hlemmur, at the eastern end of Laugavegur, or the central Lækjartorg square. They operate Mon–Sat 7am–midnight, and Sun 10am–midnight; some weekend buses run until 4am. The fare is standard ISK280 for adults (reduced for teenagers/children) and you need exact money for the ticket machine; alternatively, buy a book of tickets in advance and pay less. The Reykjavík Tourist Card gives free access to public transport in the city.

TAXIS

Widely available, many offer personalized taxi tours at fixed prices.

Hreyfill ☎ 588 5522
Borgarbíll ☎ 552 2440
BSR ☎ 561 0000
BSO (Akureyri) ☎ 461 1010

Being there

TOURIST OFFICE
Tourist Information Centre
✉ Aðalstræti 2, 101 Reykjavík
☎ 590 1550 🕐 Jun–Aug daily
8:30–6; Sep–May Mon–Fri 9–6,
Sat 10–4, Sun 10–2.

MONEY
Currency The monetary unit of Iceland is the króna, plural krónur (kr). The
international abbreviation is ISK. Notes are in denominations of 500,
1,000, 2,000 and 5,000, and coins of 1, 5, 10, 50 and 100.
Exchange Foreign currencies and travellers' cheques can be exchanged at
all banks, savings banks and bureaux de change. Credit cards are widely
accepted.

TIPPING
There is no tradition of tipping in Iceland, and giving a tip may cause
offence.

TELEPHONES
Public telephones *(sími)* are usually found outside the post office. They
take phonecards – available from post offices/telephone stations. Prepaid
GSM phonecards, for your own cell phone, from Iceland Telecom (Síminn)
and Vodafone, are available at petrol stations.

Emergency telephone numbers
Police: 112   **Ambulance:** 112
Fire: 112

International dialling codes
From Iceland to:
UK: 00 44   **USA and Canada:** 00 1
Germany: 00 49   **Netherlands:** 00 31

Patronymics

The phone book is alphabetically organized by first names as people in Iceland, from the Prime Minister down, are widely called by their given first name. Children usually take their father's name as their surname, adding 'son' or 'daughter' at the end. For example, husband and wife Jón Arnarson and Svava Stefánsdóttir could have two children, a boy and a girl, Magnús Jónsson and Erla Jónsdóttir.

POSTAL AND INTERNET SERVICES

Post offices are found in the main settlements around Iceland, and opening hours are generally Mon–Fri 9–4:30. Stamps can also be bought in most souvenir outlets where postcards are sold. Icelandic stamps are of particular interest for collectors.

A growing number of cafés in Reykjavík offer Internet access. Try the Ráðhúskaffi in the town hall, by the Tjörn, or the Icelandic Travel Market on Bankastræti. The BSÍ bus terminal on Vatnsmýrarvegur and the main tourist office also have access.

HEALTH AND SAFETY

Drugs Most pharmacies *(apótek)* have English-speaking staff.

Safe water Cold tap water is some of the cleanest and best in the world (beware of the hot, which may come from natural thermal sources and smell faintly sulphurous). In the hills, clean spring water is usually safe to drink, but avoid glacial meltwater.

Petty crime Iceland is generally a safe country with a low crime rate, although petty crime is on the increase. Leave money and valuables in the hotel safe. Carry only what you need and keep it out of sight. On Friday and Saturday nights in central Reykjavík, and Akureyri, drunkenness can be a nuisance, but the mood is usually boisterous rather than violent.

CONSULATES

UK Laufásvegur 31, Reykjavík ☎ 550 5100
Germany Laufásvegur 31, Reykjavík ☎ 530 1100
USA Laufásvegur 21, Reykjavík ☎ 562 9100

ELECTRICITY

The power supply in Iceland is 220 volts, 50HZ. Sockets accept two-pin round plugs. UK visitors require a plug adaptor and US visitors will need a transformer for appliances operating on 100–120 volts.

WHEN DEPARTING

The Flybus link to Keflavík airport leaves from Hótel Loftleiðir and other main city-centre hotels approximately 2.5 hours before each flight, (tel: 562 1011; www.flybus.is). Cost ISK1,150. Free pick-up can be arranged from major hotels and guest houses in the city. You can also check in luggage in advance – contact the number above for details. Keep any details handy for tax refunds on major purchases.

OPENING HOURS

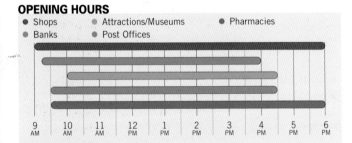

Most shops are open for a shorter time on Saturdays, often closing at 4 or earlier, but may stay open until 7pm on Fridays. Banks may stay open for longer on Thursdays and Fridays. Money exchange services in Reykjavík are available at the Tourist Information Centre, Aðalstræti 2, Jun–Aug daily 8:30–6; Sep–May Mon–Fri 9–1, 2–5, Sat 10–2.

LANGUAGE

Icelandic is directly related to Old Norse, and people with a knowledge of a Scandinavian language will have a head start. For the rest of us, it's pretty impenetrable, but a limited guide to pronunciation will help the guesswork, especially when you are trying to find your way around the country.

See page 3 for information on the Icelandic characters Ð/ð and Þ/þ. The letter j is pronounced as a y (eg Jökulsárlón). When f is before an l or n (eg Hafnarfjörður) it is pronounced as p. The letter h takes on a k-sound when in front of l, r or v (eg Hlemmur). When r is before l and n it takes on an extra d-sound (for example Perlan, which sounds like Perdlan). The double ll sounds rather like the Welsh equivalent, a soft 'kl' sound made somewhere in the back of the mouth (eg Hellnar). It's a relief to know that English is widely spoken, but even a few basic words of greeting will help to break down barriers.

Conversation

yes/no	*já/nei*	I don't speak	*ég tala ekki*
please	*gerðu það*	Icelandic	*íslensku*
thank you	*takk*	where is...?	*hvar er...?*
hello/goodbye	*hæ/bless* or *bæ*	my name is...	*ég heiti...*
good morning	*góðan daginn*	sorry	*fyrirgefið*
good evening	*gótt kvöld*	excuse me	*fyrirgefið*
I don't understand	*ég skil ekki alveg*	help!	*hjálp!*

Accommodation

hotel	*hótel*	guest house	*gistihús*
room	*herbergi*	toilet	*klósett/salerni*
single/	*fyrir einn/*	view	*útsýni*
double	*fyrir tvo*	campsite	*tjaldsvæði*

Money

bank	*banki*	credit card	*kreditkort*
exchange office	*exchange/banki*	travellers' cheque	*ferðatékki*
post office	*póstur*	passport	*vegabréf*
cash desk	*afgreiðsla*		

Food and drink

breakfast	*morgunverður*	wine/beer	*vín/bjór*
lunch	*hádegismatur*	coffee/tea	*kaffi/te*
dinner	*kvöldmatur*	water	*vatn*
restaurant	*veitingahús*	bread	*brauð*
café	*kaffihús*	fruit	*ávöxtur*
menu	*matseðill*	dessert	*eftirréttur*

Best places to see

1

Bláa Lónið (Blue Lagoon)

www.bluelagoon.com

A pool beside a power station in the middle of a windswept lava field sounds missable, but the famous Blue Lagoon is an absolute must.

It's a great way to relax and unwind from all that sightseeing. The pool is actually geothermally heated seawater, rich in natural minerals, so you feel wonderfully buoyant as you float around in the silky warmth. It's the natural by-product of the nearby Svartsengi power station, usually tactfully hidden in clouds of steam, and uses water straight from 2,000m (6,560ft) below the ground, which is at a much higher temperature. Once it has cooled down, the water is the comfortable temperature of a hot bath and you can simply lie back in the open air and think of Iceland – even if it's snowing on your head! The opacity comes from the natural white silica mud mixed with minerals and an algae, which gives it the trade-mark milky blue colour, whatever the weather. Buckets of soapy white gunge are placed around the margins – it's a pleasant sludge of the silica and minerals and you can smear it over yourself for glorious exfoliation. It's supposed to be good for skin conditions (there's a special pool dedicated to psoriasis sufferers, who find great relief) and you'll certainly come away with silky-feeling skin.

The bottom is comfortable sand and the water gets no deeper than adult shoulder-height, so nonswimmers can feel confident. However children under the age of 11 must be supervised. There's always a lifeguard on duty, fully clothed against the elements as it's much colder in the air than in the water. Take your towel to the lagoon entrance – you need to dry off before returning to the changing rooms. Book ahead for a spa massage, or simply stand under the waterfall for a natural, shoulder-pounding massage in the main pool.

✚ 17L ✉ 5km (3 miles) from Grindavík, off Route 43, 45 minutes southwest of Reykjavík ☎ 420 8800 🕐 All year, daily ✋ Moderate 🍴 Blue Café (£). Lava restaurant caters for larger numbers (£–££) 🚌 Regular service from main bus station in Reykjavík, also calls in at bigger hotels on request ❓ You can hire swimsuits, bathrobes and towels. Take shampoo ℹ Tourist Information, Icelandic Saltfish Museum, Hafnargata 12a, Grindavík ☎ 420 1190

2 Flatey

This beautiful island in Breiðafjörður Bay is one of the prettiest spots in Iceland and an unexpected secret makes it well worth the effort to get there.

Its name tells you there are no exciting natural features in store – Flatey simply means 'flat island', and as you walk up from the harbour there is nothing especially remarkable about the old wooden houses grouped there, gracious and appealing though they are. Take the well-trodden track that leads through the grassy meadowland, bursting with buttercups and patrolled by anxious Arctic terns, which nest on the ground here in large numbers. Look carefully and you may spot the downy grey chicks, but mind your head – the terns can peck you hard and sharp if they think you're getting too close.

This way leads to the wooden church, deceptively modest in its simple lines, but the interior is like no other. Most Lutheran churches are free of embellishment, but this one has been painted with a rich set of frescoes, depicting local folk in biblical settings. The effect is breathtaking. The brushstrokes are bold and black, the figures vivid and engaging – note a young, unmistakably Icelandic 'Christ the Fisherman' over the altar. The murals are the work of a Spanish–Icelandic painter, Baltasar Samper, who came here in the 1960s and worked for his keep over a period of several years.

The church is not the only surprise on this extraordinary island. Tucked just behind it is a tiny wooden shed – peer through the murky windows and you'll recognize the smallest and oldest library in Iceland, a legacy of Flatey's historic importance as a trading and religious centre. One of the great medieval manuscripts, *Flateyjarbók*, was held here until its dispersal to Denmark – it's now in the Culture House in Reykjavík.

The cosy Hótel Flatey (£££, tel: 422 7610; www.hotelflatey.is), in restored houses in the tiny village, makes a stopover here very comfortable.

➕ 3D 📧 Middle of Breiðafjörður Bay 🍴 Small restaurant Veitingastofan Vogur (£–££) 🚢 Ferry Baldur from Stykkishólmur calls in daily ☎ 438 1454; www.seatours.is

❓ Look out for white-tailed sea eagles around the islands of Breiðafjörður

3 Gullfoss and Geysir

Two of Iceland's most spectacular and famous natural sights are found within a few kilometres of each other near the head of a great valley.

Gullfoss is the 'golden waterfall' on the River Hvítá, the most outstandingly beautiful in this land of tumbling water. You can usually see the cloud of vapour and hear the roar long before you see it, set sideways on at the top of a long, narrow gorge which reaches depths of 70m (230ft). It is in fact two falls, one immediately above the other and at right angles to it, so you get double the effect. You can view the falls from the railed-off point above or take the path that leads right down to the water, but be warned – you're liable to get wet just from the spray there!

It's hard to imagine anybody wanting to destroy this wonder of nature, but in 1907 it came under threat from developers who sought to contain it for hydroelectric power. They were opposed by a young woman, Sigríður Tómasdóttir, from the neighbouring farm of Brattholt, and her campaign to save the waterfall and its gorge was ultimately successful. She's known as the heroine of the falls and her statue stands by the visitor centre.

In contrast, the spouting steam vents on the hillside at Geysir (pronounced 'gayzeer') have been valued since they first appeared in the 13th century, but the original great Geysir, which gave its name to the phenomenon, no longer blows. It was probably blocked over the centuries by eager sightseers, who threw debris into the bubbling pool to accelerate the spouting. More recent moves to replumb it have damaged it beyond repair. Geysir's smaller neighbour Strokkur is well worth seeing in its own right, and goes off every ten minutes or so, shooting boiling steam some 30m (100ft) into the air (make sure you stand up-wind). It's fascinating to watch as the water in the circular pool at its base is sucked in and out by the pressure of hot geothermal water and cold river water down below, as though you were standing on the back of a living being rather than stone. When the pool is almost full, the water at the centre suddenly bubbles up in a luminous blue swell and the plume of steam erupts with a great hiss – not to be missed.

✚ 20J (Geysir), 21J (Gullfoss) ✉ 125km (78 miles) east of Reykjavík, on Route 35 🕙 Open access 🖐 Free; small charge for multimedia presentation at visitor centre 🍴 Hotels, restaurant and coffee shop at Geysir; café at Gullfoss 🚌 Both sites, classic Golden Circle coach tours, half day or whole day 🛈 Geyser Centre ☎ 480 6800; www.gullfoss.is

4 Hallgrímskirkja, Reykjavík

www.hallgrimskirkja.is

Like a giant space shuttle about to take off, the dramatic white tower of the Hallgrímskirkja looms over the old-town district of Reykjavík.

Completed in 1974, the church took some 30 years to build, and locals are still getting used to it, but – love it or hate it – you won't get far away from it, for it seems to watch you down every street. It's the most striking modern building in Iceland, designed by Guðjón Samúelsson (1887–1950), and is named after the 17th-century hymn-writer and poet Reverend Hallgrímur Pétursson. It actually stands at the top of Skólavörðustígur and, by the time you have panted your way up the hill, you'll find this a breathtaking building in more senses than one.

While rockets come to mind when you see the church from a distance, close-up its concrete pillars resemble giant hexagonal volcanic columns, or even a fantastical set of organ pipes. Step through the door and it is like being inside a towering ice-cathedral, very cool and unadorned, grey and white, with narrow gothic windows of clear glass showing strips of sky. Turn around and you'll see the huge organ, vulgar by comparison – it boasts 5,275 steely pipes, each sponsored by members of the congregation. The simple furnishings you might expect of a Lutheran church here become minimalist and very stylish. They include a hexagonal font of clear rock crystal, made in the Czech Republic, and mounted on a block of Icelandic rock. You can take the lift to the 8th floor of the tower, 73m (239ft) high, for a panorama over the rooftops of Reykjavík. Restoration of the concrete facing means major building work will continue through 2009.

The heroic statue in front of the Hallgrímskirkja is of Leifur Eiríksson, credited with the first European discovery of America around AD1000 (➤ 11).

 Reykjavík 4d ✉ Skólavörðuholt ☎ 510 1000 Church May–Sep daily 9–6; Oct–Apr daily 9–5. Tower daily 10–5 Tower inexpensive 🚌 7 ❓ Service Sun 11am. Frequent organ recitals Jul and Aug
ℹ Tourist Information Centre, Aðalstræti 2
☎ 590 1550

5 Jökulsárgljúfur

The narrow strip of Jökulsárgljúfur encompasses a magnificent valley, a deep gorge, mysterious echoing rocks and Europe's most powerful waterfall.

The park follows the canyon formed by the Jökulsá á Fjöllum, one of the major rivers, which churns northwards from Vatnajökull (► 154). It is believed that the canyon was originally formed in the course of a few days, following an explosion of the volcano and subsequent release of meltwater *(jökulhlaup)*.

At the park's southern end is Dettifoss, a massive waterfall 45m (147ft) high and 100m (328ft) wide, over which the river pours at an incredible rate. It's glacial meltwater, so it's filthy –

this is not a pretty waterfall but its power is awesome. You can hear the roar some distance away and when you stand next to it the effect is shattering to the senses (be careful, there are no barriers). There's a footpath down the western side, back to Ásbyrgi, which takes two days to complete, and as you work your way downstream you'll see smaller falls at Hafragilsfoss and Selfoss. There are plenty of short walks in the area – information is available from the ranger stations at Ásbyrgi and Vesturdalur.

The half-way point of the canyon is Hólmatungur, lush and green and full of wild flowers in summer. Further north, the strange craggy rocks of Hljóðaklettar, near the Vesturdalur campsite, are famous for their echoes. The northern end of the park at Ásbyrgi is also its most accessible point. Here the canyon opens into a beautiful wide horseshoe-shaped valley, reputedly a hoofprint left behind by the god Odin's horse Sleipnir. The high walls protect a basin full of birch and rowan trees, with an outcrop, Eyjan, floating in the middle, a perfect island in a sea of green.

✚ 12C ✉ Main entrance from Kelduhverfið, west of Ásbyrgi ☎ 465 2195 (National Park information); www.ust.is ♿ Access is limited by the state of the roads, open only in summer 🎫 Free 🍴 Café at Ásbyrgi petrol station ❓ Access roads to west (F862) and east (864). Keep to west for Hljóðaklettar, but road deteriorates to jeep track south of Dettifoss

ℹ Tourist Information Centre, Hafnarstræti 82, Akureyri ☎ 550 0720

6 Jökulsárlón

www.jokulsarlon.is

Icebergs of extraordinary age and beauty float on this glacial lagoon, separated from the sea by only a narrow slip of land.

After the monotony of the surrounding landscape and the coal-black of the *sandur* (glacial gravel) shore, the luminous beauty of the icebergs at Jökulsárlón always surprises. Even on a grey day the compressed ancient turquoise ice, humbug-striped with black glacial moraine, seems to be lit from within as the bergs move in a stately slow dance in the wind. The little that shows on the surface can seem as big as a house, and the view shifts subtly from hour to hour. They are calves of the great Breiðamerkur glacier which looms up behind, its snout stained black with lava grit. It has been flowing down these mountains for centuries and, as photos in the little café show, it has grown and retreated over the years, gouging a lake 100m (320ft) deep with icy waters that pour through into the sea. It is in danger of breaking through altogether one day, sweeping Route 1 and the fragile suspension bridge with it.

There are good points for photography on both sides of the bridge, and it's worth taking the amphibious vehicle tour down into the lake to get close among the icebergs. You can often see seals fishing in the swift channel, while eider ducks swim fearlessly between the shifting ice blocks, and in summer the air is electric with the sharp cries of Arctic terns. If the tour buses spoil your view, then Breiðarlón is another iceberg lagoon to the south, easily accessed on foot from the main road.

➕ 26K ✉ Just off Route 1, 75km (47 miles) west of Höfn
🕐 Open access ✋ Free 🍴 Small visitor centre and café on site, open mid-May to mid-Sep 🚤 Amphibious vehicles tour the lake (tel: 478 2222)
ℹ Tourist Information Centre, Hafnarbraut 30, Höfn
☎ 478 1500

Mývatn

Birds in their thousands come to nest in this conservation area of water and greenery set in an active geothermal area.

It is said that more duck species breed here than anywhere else in the world, 15 in total, including the colourful harlequin, Barrow's goldeneye, scaup and tufted and long-tailed ducks. You'll also find whooper swans, Slavonian grebes and both red-throated and great northern divers. Their breeding ground is mostly to the west of the lake and this area is closed to traffic in high summer.

The birds are part of an ecosystem based on the millions of midges and flies which give the lake its name (pronounced meevatn) and also provide food for salmon and char. Their microscopic skeletons have gathered on the lake bottom and support a different economy – diatomite processing in a factory east of Reykjahlíð, for use in industrial filters, fertilizer and paint.

The lake averages a depth of only 2.5m (8.2ft) and covers some 37sq km (14sq miles). It's in a shallow depression and is full of small green islands. These include many 'pseudo-craters' – looking like mini-volcanoes, they are actually the result of gas explosions under the lava. Extensive

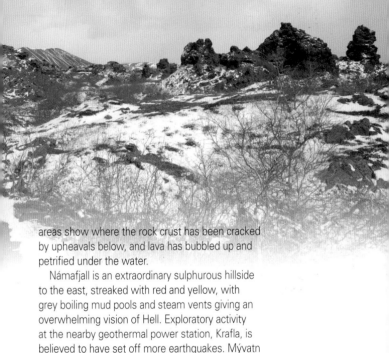

areas show where the rock crust has been cracked by upheavals below, and lava has bubbled up and petrified under the water.

Námafjall is an extraordinary sulphurous hillside to the east, streaked with red and yellow, with grey boiling mud pools and steam vents giving an overwhelming vision of Hell. Exploratory activity at the nearby geothermal power station, Krafla, is believed to have set off more earthquakes. Mývatn has its own 'Blue Lagoon', the **Nature Baths,** offering summer bathing until midnight.

➕ 11D ✉ 99km (61 miles) east of Akureyri 🆔 Open access 🍴 Several cafés and restaurants around Reykjahlíð (£–£££) ❓ The midges can get in your nose, ears, mouth and hair, so a netted hat is recommended for Jun and Aug. Hire a bicycle for leisurely exploration ☎ 464 4240, 464 4103

🈯 Tourist Information Centre, Hraunvegur 8
☎ 464 4390; www.visitmyvatn.is
Nature Baths
☎ 464 4411; www.naturebaths.com

8 Skaftafell

Approaching Skaftafell National Park from the west, a panorama of green hills, tumbling ice and gothic mountain pinnacles fills your view.

As you get closer, the scene resolves into three deeply crevassed glaciers, with Skaftafellsjökull flanked by Morsárjökull to the left and Svínafellsjökull to the right, and a fourth, Skeiðarárjökull, much broader and flatter in appearance, over to your left. They are tributaries of the great ice caps of Vatnajökull and Öræfajökull. You can follow the path up to the snout of Skaftafellsjökull, which pours down into a scenic lake surrounded by surprisingly lush vegetation, but be careful near the glacier where slippery clay overlays the ice under foot. If you want to walk on

the glacier itself, make use of the expert ranger service which offers properly guided excursions, hikes and rock climbing.

Sheltered by the mountains, this site gets more than its fair share of good weather but can also catch the rain. The campsite is a very popular place at weekends and so you may prefer to dodge the crowds and come midweek. In summer the rounded hill behind the visitor centre, Skorar, is covered in birch woods and heath, and there are beautiful walks to the dramatic waterfall of Svartifoss (► 60) and into the next valley and the mountains behind. The woods are full of twittering redwings. Keep an eye open too for Iceland's smallest bird, a wren *(troglodytes islandicus)*, slightly larger than its mainland European cousin.

The braided gravel plain below Skaftafell was the scene of a massive *jökulhlaup* in 1996, when the volcano Grímsvötn erupted beneath Vatnajökull and the resulting flood waters swept away roads and bridges. Trucks and diggers, toy-sized in this vast landscape, constantly shift the gravel around in attempts to limit future damage.

➕ 25K ✉ 327km (203 miles) east of Reykjavík 🕐 Open access 🍴 Café at visitor centre (£) ✋ Free ❓ Mountain guide service ☎ 478 1627, 894 2959
ℹ Visitor Centre 🕐 May–Sep ☎ 478 1627

9 Þingvellir

www.thingvellir.is

Iceland formed the first parliamentary democracy in the world at Þingvellir (Thingvellir), setting a system of government that would last for centuries. It is now a UNESCO World Heritage Site.

The great fault line at Þingvellir, where the geological plates of America and Europe are tearing slowly apart, provided a remarkable natural arena for the gatherings of freemen, chieftains and bishops to discuss matters of law and justice, crime and punishment. The first Alþing, or parliament, was held here in AD930 and they continued annually (with some breaks) until 1789, when the plain fell 1m (3ft) in an earthquake and the power base shifted to Reykjavík. The Lawspeaker recited from memory one third of the country's laws each time. You can stand at his rock, marked with a flagpole and wooden platform, and survey the plain below where men would have gathered in temporary turf booths for two weeks each summer for the social event of the year. Sound echoes off the long line of sheer cliffs behind, making for excellent acoustics.

Birch and willow grow amid the fissured rocks of the plain, with the lake to the south and low mountains in the distance, and the eye is drawn to the 19th-century church and the white-gabled farmhouse beside it. The classic view of the site is from the hill above and to the west, just off Route 36. By the approach to the church, one of the fissures of cold, clear water has become an oracle, with coins gleaming like fishscales at the bottom – ask your question as your coin falls and, if you can see it land on the bottom, the answer is 'yes'.

➕ 19K ✉ 49km (30 miles) northeast of Reykjavík on Route 361 🕐 Open access 💲 Free 🍴 Café (£) at visitor centre 🚤 Summer boat trips and fishing on the lake, book at visitor centre ❓ Good walk along chasm from the visitor centre by Hótel Valhöll, past Lawspeaker's Rock and the drowning pool Drekkingarhylor to Öxarárfoss waterfall ℹ Visitor Centre for National Park, junction of routes 36 and 361 ☎ 482 2660

10 Vestmannaeyjar (Westmann Islands)

www.vestmannaeyjar.is

This intriguing archipelago off the southwest coast includes Surtsey, a new island, and Heimaey, which suffered a devastating eruption in 1973.

The low black wedge of Surtsey emerged from the sea in a spew of flames and ash between 1963 and 1966, the result of a submarine volcano on the same great faultline which is splitting the mainland. The island is protected so that scientists may study the growth and colonization of an island which reflects the creation of Iceland itself. Already small plants have taken root and even the first earthworm has been found.

Despite their settled appearance, none of the Westmann Islands is older than 5–10,000 years (infantile in geological terms) and parts of the biggest and only inhabited island, Heimaey (pronounced haymay), are a lot newer than that. The eruption of the volcano here on 23 January 1973 took everybody by surprise. By great luck, the fishing fleet was in and so the population of 5,000 was evacuated safely that same night. Then began an epic battle to prevent the town being totally destroyed by lava, which continued to flow for five months; seawater was pumped over it and you can see clearly how the flow stopped just short of the harbour. In fact, the new rock narrowed the harbour mouth to make it one of the safest anchorages in Iceland.

The gritty lava on Eldfell is still warm to the touch, and hot enough below the surface to bake bread – you can climb it for a great view over the town and of the green amphitheatre of Herjólfsdalur, where locals have their own three-day mega-party in early August. Look out for puffin hunters on the cliffs opposite the harbour. Their selective catch makes little dent on the population.

➕ 20M ✉ 11km (7 miles) off south coast 🍴 Various places on Heimaey (£–£££) 🚢 Ferry from Þorlákshöfn takes 3 hours ☎ 481 2800 ✈ Flights from Reykjavík and Bakki to Heimaey; also sightseeing flights over Surtsey
ℹ Tourist Information Centre, Ráðhúströð, Heimaey
☎ 481 3555

Best things to do

Good places to have lunch

Bautinn (£–££)
Unfussy, with the best hamburgers in town (➤ 140).
✉ Hafnarstræti 92, Akureyri ☎ 462 1818

Bláa Kannan (£)
Lunch in stylish surroundings – and leave room for cake (➤ 140).
✉ Hafnarstræti 96, Akureyri ☎ 461 4600

Café Iða (£–££)
Relax with a coffee and a gateau or savoury snack in this stylish
café above the Iða bookshop.
✉ Lækjargata 2a, Reykjavík ☎ 511 5001

Café Paris (£)
Bag a window seat, or dine al fresco if the sun's shining (➤ 112).
✉ Austervöllur, Reykjavík ☎ 551 1020

Café Sólon (£)
Great for a mid-shopping snack (➤ 113).
✉ Bankastræti 7A, Reykjavík ☎ 562 3232

Fylgifiskar (£–££)
There are just a few tables in this fabulous fish shop (► 114), open Monday to Friday (Saturday in winter).
✉ Skólavörðustígur 8, Reykjavík ☎ 533 1303; www.fylgifiskar.is

Gamli Baukur (£–££)
Set right on the harbour, where it's all happening (► 141).
✉ Húsavík ☎ 464 2442

Kaffi Hornið (£–££)
Simple food, well cooked (► 155).
✉ Hafnarbraut 42, Höfn ☎ 478 2600

Sushismiðjan (£–££)
Fresh sushi to take away or eat just outside on the harbour.
✉ Geirsgata 3, Reykjavík ☎ 517 3366; www.sushimidjan.is

Svarta Kaffið (£–££)
The home-made soup *in* a bread roll is a special winter warmer (► 115).
✉ Laugavegur 54, Reykjavík ☎ 551 2999

Top activities

Aerial sightseeing For a bird's-eye view of volcanoes and glaciers, Eagle Air (Flugfélagið Ernir) offer sightseeing flights from the airport in Reykjavík. The clear air means visibility can be pin-sharp, giving a great overview of the country. **Eagle Air** ☎ 562 4200

Birdwatching The concentration of nesting birds in Iceland makes it a paradise for birdwatchers. The main season for migrants is mid-May to mid-Aug, and two of the best places to see them are Mývatn (➤ 46–47) and Látrabjarg (➤ 103). If you're serious, try specialist tour operator **Naturetrek** ✉ Cheriton Mill, Cheriton, Alresford, Hampshire, SO24 0NG, UK ☎ 01962 733051; www.naturetrek.co.uk

Cycling Cycling around Iceland can be a bit of a challenge, with bumpy and unmade roads, and unpredictable weather. Sandstorms can be a hazard in the south. Still, people like to do it. Contact local tourist offices for information about cycle hire, and if you bring your own, bring spare parts.

Dolphin- and whale-spotting Several sites around Iceland offer facilities for this, and Húsavík is probably the best, but similar trips are offered from Reykjavík and other coastal settlements.
North Sailing ✉ Húsavík ☎ 464 7272; www.northsailing.is
Reykjavík Whale Watching ✉ Ægisgarður 7 ☎ 555 3565; www.elding.is

Fishing With over 100 salmon rivers, 20 of them world-ranked, Iceland offers great sport fishing from mid-June to mid-September; but the best places are not cheap. Sea angling is also popular. Contact local tourist offices about opportunities and permits.
Icelandic Travel Market (➤ 29)

Hiking There's good local information and mapping to help you plan hiking routes in Iceland. The terrain, particularly in the interior, can be harsh, and weather conditions change very quickly, so seek expert advice on the correct equipment depending on your route and time of travel. The land is fragile, so camping outside official sites is discouraged, but there are more than 100 campsites to choose from. See local tourist offices for listings.

Horse-riding Icelandic horses are small, surefooted and very comfortable to ride. The 'fifth gait' with head held high, unique to these horses, is much smoother than a bumpy trot and not as fast as a rollicking canter. Treks can be arranged to suit any ability and get you out into the wilds. **Ishestar Riding Tours** ☎ 555 7000; www.ishestar.is. **Skipalækur** by Egilsstaðir ☎ 471 1324

Swimming A ready supply of cheap hot water means that Iceland boasts more outdoor public swimming pools per head than the rest of Europe put together. The standard is high, entry prices low and there are often bubbling 'hot-pots' and water chutes. Akureyri has one of the finest, but you'll find them in just about every town and settlement, often open until 8 or 9pm.

Winter sports There's not enough good snow for a lot of top-class skiing in Iceland, but the best is found in the north around Akureyri (www.hlidarfjall.is), which also has a skating rink. Skidoos offer transport over the snowcaps all year round and trips are available around all the main glaciers. The snowmobiles are easy to operate and fun, if rather noisy and smelly, and can get you high into the wilds quickly – but stick close to your guide as there is a real danger of crevasses, especially in the summer. For advice on the best packages, contact the Reykjavík tourist office (► 28).

around Skaftafell

Two walks lead from the visitor centre: a short one to the glacier, and this longer one to the waterfall of Svartifoss.

Walk towards the campsite, and bear right along the gravel path. Take the signed path to Svartifoss uphill, zigzagging through low birch and willow. Keep on the main path, cross a wooden bridge and climb the side of the gorge to reach the high Hundarfoss waterfall. Where the path branches, keep right up the slope.

There are good views behind you over the plain, with rivers braiding across the gravel towards the sea. You can also see the broad snout of Skeiðarárjökull to the east.

Pass the smaller waterfall, Magnúsarfoss, and keep right, following signs for Svartifoss. Continue across an open area of moss, heather and crowberries.

Svartifoss, down to your left, appears as a dramatic black gash in the hillside. Columnar basalt forms an echoing natural amphitheatre of hanging columns, like organ pipes, surrounding the central water plume. The pointed mountain ahead is Skarðatindur, 1,385m (4,543ft) high.

Follow the precipitous path, which can be slippery, down to falls.

Enjoy a drink of the clear water and picnic on the rocks.

Scramble over the stepping stones and climb the rocky path – red-paint markers show the way. Turn up the steep hill, signed to Kristianartinder.

It's worth the long haul up for the views of the mountains from the viewing table.

Head back downhill, past the finger post, following signs to Lambhagi. Continue downhill and keep left at a fork. Soon bear left, signed Lambhagi. Turn left and cross the stream above Magnúsarfoss. Retrace your steps down the main path back to the visitor centre.

Distance 4km (2.5 miles)
Time Allow two hours, longer with a picnic stop
Start/end point A circular walk; start from the National Park Visitor Centre ✚ 25K
Lunch Take a picnic to eat at the falls

Places to take the children

The Fræðasetrið Nature Centre, Sandgerði

This popular centre on the western tip of Reykjanes promises 'instruction, exhibits, fun and adventure on land and sea', with everything from sailing to storytelling.

✉ Garðvegur 1 ☎ 423 7551; www.sandgerdi.is 🕓 Mon–Fri 9–5, Sat–Sun 1–5 ✋ Inexpensive

Hafnarfjörður

Rapidly developing as the Viking capital of Iceland, Hafnarfjörður has not only a fantastic Viking restaurant on the harbourfront, including some life-sized models outside and a fascinating interior, but also an entire Viking 'village' (➤ 93), where craftsmen can be seen at work in the West Nordic Cultural House.

Hafnarfjörður is also known as the Icelandic home of elves, who are thought to live in the rocks here. There are popular guided walks around the elf settlements of the town.

Information and bookings ☎ 694 2785; www.alfar.is

Hvalamiðstöðin (Whale Museum), Húsavík

Good pictorial information helps
to identify the main species:
there are real whale skeletons so
you get an idea of their size, and
an amazing 'touch table' where
you can compare the feel of
whaleskin and sharkskin. There is
also a section dedicated to Keiko,
killer-whale star of the *Free Willy*
films, including a life-sized model.

✉ Hafnarstétt ☎ 464 2520

Icelandic Aviation Museum, Akureyri

The country's biggest collection of historic aircraft is located in a
hangar by Akureyri airport. There's a flight simulator, an Auster V
ambulance aircraft and artefacts from an RAF Fairey Battle aircraft
which crashed near here in 1941.

✉ Hringteigur 5 ☎ 461 4400; www.flugsafn.is 🕐 Jun–Aug daily 1–5

Reykjavík Family Park and Zoo

This lively summer theme park and play area on a Viking theme
has an informal zoo including local species such as Icelandic
horses, Arctic foxes and reindeer. Various activities for older kids
include electric cars and diggers. Café, toilets and changing
facilities on site. There's also a great swimming pool close by.

✉ Laugardalur park ☎ 575 7800; www.mu.is 🕐 Summer 10–6; winter 10–5
✋ Inexpensive

The Volcano Show, Reykjavík

Daily film shows of erupting volcanoes and earthquakes make a
great introduction to the geology and landscape of Iceland. Films are
shown year-round in the Red Rock Cinema, in several languages.

✉ Hellusundi 6a ☎ 845 9548

Reykjavík nightlife

In Reykjavík and other main centres, innocent cafés by day turn into pubs and clubs at night. Friday and Saturday are the big nights, but they don't start to get going until midnight. Note that smoking is banned in all public areas, including bars and clubs.

Boston
Lively bar and latest venture of the owner of the once-legendary Sirkus.
✉ Laugavegur 28b ☎ 517 7816

Broadway
Just out of the town centre, this disco in Hótel Ísland is said to be the biggest in Iceland. Live music and cabaret. Dress code.
✉ Ármúli 9 ☎ 533 1100; www.broadway.is

The Dubliner
Every city has an Irish theme pub, and Reykjavík is no exception. Locals say it was imported from the Emerald Isle (complete with staff) on the back of a lorry.
✉ Hafnarstræti 4 ☎ 511 3232

Glaumbar
A sporty bar near the old harbour that likes to turn up the music.
✉ Tryggvagata 20 ☎ 552 6868

Hverfisbarinn
Located at the National Theatre, this is a café by day and lively bar in the evening.
✉ Hverfisgata 20 ☎ 699 1105

Kaffi Reykjavík Ice Bar
A good pub atmosphere in a large old building near the harbour. Dancing and live music at weekends.
✉ Vesturgata 2 ☎ 552 3030

Kaffibarinn

A trendy spot for posers and wannabes. Between Laugavegur and Skólavörðustígur.

✉ Bergstaðastræti 1 ☎ 551 1588

Nasa

Bills itself as the biggest nightclub in the centre of the capital; popular with all ages.

✉ Austurvöllur ☎ 511 1313; www.nasa.is

Prikið

One of the city's oldest – and smallest – bars, this is a popular choice with the student crowd.

✉ Bankastræti 12 ☎ 511 2866

Skuggabarinn

In the smart Hótel Borg, this is where the well-dressed dance the night away.

✉ Pósthusstræti 11 ☎ 551 1440

Sólon

Restaurant and gallery by day, bar by night, where the arty crowd hang out.

✉ Bankastræti 7a ☎ 562 3232;
www.solon.is

Tunglið

Live music is promised every night at this popular club. Spot the up-and-coming musicians on weekdays, and enjoy the well-established bands at weekends.

✉ Tryggvagata 22 ☎ 517 2277

Places to shop

Reykjavík Laugavegur is Reykjavík's famous shopping street, with lots of high-class designer fashion, hand-crafted jewellery, two great book stores (with books and magazines in all languages, not just Icelandic) and small cafés. Several shops cater exclusively for babies and toddler fashion – cute, but not cheap. For unusual designer jewellery, look out for Gullkúnst Helgu. If you want more exclusive designer clothes, jewellery and art and antiques shops, try Skólavörðustígur.

Elsewhere, for Icelandic crafts try the Rammagerðin Icelandic Giftstore on Laugavegur and Hafnarstræti, which stocks treasures from designer glassware to handmade wooden toys; the Traveller Shop on Bankastræti for maps, guides and novelties; and for gifts, jewellery and top-class woollens, historic Thorvaldsens Bazar (on the corner of Aðalstræti and Austurstræti) has a great selection – shop profits have supported children's charities for years. 12 Tonár, on Skólavörðustígur, is the place for Icelandic music, from Hjálmar and Sigur Rós to Hallbjörn Hjartarson, the 'Icelandic singing cowboy'. For top value, Álafoss, north of town in Mosfellsbær, is a factory outlet with woollens and other high-quality souvenirs.

Kringlan is the city's showpiece shopping mall, with more than 150 outlets – you can buy anything here from classy Swedish homeware to modern art. It's set away from the town centre but with a free car park underneath, and easy bus access. Find the latest fashions in Noa Noa, Boss and the three floors of Galleri Sautján.

For outdoor gear try 66°N, which has been an Icelandic institution since 1926. Íslandia sells a wide range of souvenirs, from knitwear to lava candle-holders. The upper floor has a choice of fast-food outlets, including a Hard Rock Café. The Smáralind shopping mall in Kópavogur includes some good boutiques among its more ordinary shops and international names such as Debenhams and Benetton.

If you want to take some Icelandic delicacies home with you, try the weekend market in Kolaportiđ, on Tryggvagata – it has everything from pancakes to great sides of smoked salmon, and you can often taste before you buy.

Akureyri also offers good shopping, though on a smaller scale. The main shopping street is pedestrianized Hafnarstræti, with a branch of the Eymundsson book and stationery store on the corner. Fold-Anna is a factory outlet for beautiful woollen goods, including capes, blankets and hats. Listflèttan stocks some unusual and quality ceramics and art prints. Amarohúsiđ is a wide-ranging department store. For souvenirs, the Viking shop has a good range. High fashion is found along Skipagata, with trendy designer outlets such as Perfect. Gleratorg is the town's shopping mall.

Tax-free shopping Visitors are entitled to reclaim 15 per cent on purchases of more than ISK4,000 made at any shop displaying the 'tax-free' symbol. You pay the full price at the checkout, but ask and you'll be given a form to fill in. Hand this in at the airport bank when you leave, showing the goods as proof, to obtain your refund – the saving is well worth it. You do not have to show woollen goods in this way. FOREX Bank, at Bankastræti 2, and the Tourist Information Centre, at Ađalstræti 2, can also refund tax for you.

Christmas every day Don't miss Jólagarđurinn, the red-painted house where it's Christmas every day, just out beyond Kjarnaskógar, east of Akureyri. It's stuffed with beautiful Christmas items, including traditional Icelandic decorations. You can picnic in the garden, alongside a whimsical wishing tree and fairytale tower.

Exploring

Iceland lies just below the Arctic Circle, and is a relatively new country, both in geological terms and habitation. Settlers arrived here from Norway only towards the end of the first century, and natural disasters, including volcanic eruptions, climate change, plague and trade embargoes all played a part in keeping the population low. Today some 300,000 people live here (60 per cent in the greater Reykjavík area, with Akureyri the only other city of any size) and in the last hundred or so years, their prosperity has increased dramatically. Most Icelanders enjoy a high standard of living, often holding down several jobs in order to maintain this. Nevertheless, there's a relaxed attitude to life, with little crime. The Icelandic language is related to Old Norse, proudly maintained in the face of globalization, and largely impenetrable to non-Scandinavians. English and Danish are also widely spoken.

Reykjavík and the West

This area encompasses a little of just about everything Iceland has to offer.

The west of Iceland stretches from the majestic Snæfellsnes mountain ridge and the flatter lava flow of the Reykjanes peninsula, to the the deeply indented older rock of the West Fjords, which form the northwest tip of Europe. To the south, the fertile floodplain of the Ölfusá and Þjórsa (Thórsa) rivers marks one end of the great geological rift which splits Iceland in two and spat up the Westmann Islands. The early settlers made their home here, and there are important centres of history at Þingvellir (Thingvellir), Reykholt and, of course, the capital, Reykjavík.

Reykjavík

REYKJAVÍK

Iceland's capital city is pleasingly unique. In the haphazard streets around the old harbour, the colourful old painted buildings of wood and tin give it the appearance of a frontier town, and are a reminder that Reykjavík barely appeared on the map before the end of the 18th century. It has no grand buildings like other European capitals, for Iceland was a poor country before the last century.

But the unsophisticated, homely feel is deceptive: the locals publish and read more books per head than anywhere else in the world, and they embrace new technological gadgetry with an enthusiasm that borders on the obsessive and leaves bigger, more entrenched countries of Europe lumbering in their wake. Paradoxically, they work long hours and hard (often with extra summer jobs) to maintain an admirably high standard of living; yet they retain a broad world view and a laid-back attitude to life, a healthy resistance to authority, a sense of fun and mischief; they drink to get drunk and are sentimental about a country small enough to behave like a community.

There's plenty to enjoy here on a short break, with surprisingly good shopping, excellent restaurants and lots of good small museums and galleries to explore which are dominated by 20th-century art. The famous nightlife kicks off on Fridays and Saturdays around 11pm and nobody goes home before 5am.

Temperatures are generally mild; around freezing point in winter, 11°C (52°F) in summer. In the clear, constant light of a summer's evening, Reykjavík's a fascinating place. On a snowy winter's night, with candlelight glowing through every window, it's enchanting.

www.visitreykjavik.is

🗝 18K ❓ City sightseeing bus tours operate Jun–Aug; www.city-sightseeing.com

ℹ️ Tourist Information, The Centre, Aðalstræti 2, 101 Reykjavík ☎ 590 1550

Árbæjarsafn (Reykjavík City Museum)

For a glimpse into lives of the past, this open-air museum site is nosy parkers' heaven. Since 1957, interesting old houses have been migrating – lock, stock and barrel – from the centre of Reykjavík to form a unique historical collection to the east of the city. The original farmstead of Árbær, with its turf roof, has been joined by buildings of timber, stone and iron-cladding from all across Iceland. The church, which was brought here from Skagafjörður, dates from 1842 and is a picturesque spot for summer wedding parties. You can go into many of the houses to enjoy the period furnishings; often you feel that the real owner has just slipped into the next room. Traditional craft days bring the old skills to life – join in the haymaking and butter-churning and watch the blacksmith at work.

www.reykjavikmuseum.is

✚ *Heykjavík 8b (off map)* ✉ Kistuhylur 4 ☎ 411 6300

🕔 Jun–Aug daily 10–5; regular afternoon tours in winter

✋ Inexpensive 🚌 12, 24 ❓ Look for demonstrations and craft days. Milking takes place at 4:30 every day. Guided tours in winter Mon, Wed, Fri 1–2

Ásmundarsafn (Ásmundur Sveinsson Sculpture Gallery)

The extraordinary whitewashed building with its golf-ball dome, likened to an igloo, was designed and built in the 1940s by the artist as his home and studio. It's now a museum dedicated to him, but his work is at its most impressive in the outdoor sculpture garden. Sveinsson (1893–1982) studied in Copenhagen and Paris and became one of Iceland's leading popular sculptors. He took his inspiration from the sagas, nature and the oddities of people in everyday life, and his abstract work explores a variety of styles. You'll recognize his distinctively bold and primitive forms everywhere.

www.listasafnreykjavikur.is

✚ *Reykjavík 8d* ✉ Sigtún ☎ 553 2155 🕐 May–Sep daily 10–4; Oct–Apr daily 1–4 ✋ Free 🚍 2, 15, 17, 19 ❓ Part of Reykjavík Art Museum

Austurvöllur

This peaceful leafy square, surrounded by shops and restaurants, lies at the heart of the old town on the site where Ingólfur Arnarson, the man known as the First Settler, had his hay meadows in around AD874 – the name means 'east field'. Given this historical provenance, it is entirely appropriate that the modest grey stone Alþingishús (parliament building) of 1881 should form the southern side. Some 63 MPs meet in the modern building next door from Monday to Thursday, with a Prime Minister and an elected president at their head. The statue in the centre of the square is of Jón Sigurðsson (1811–79), hero of the call for independence from Denmark in 1855; in his honour, National (Independence) Day is celebrated on 17 June (➤ 22), his birthday. The elegant little Dómkirkjan with its square tower is the Lutheran cathedral, built in 1796. Hótel Borg, along the east side, is Iceland's oldest and most splendid hotel.

➕ *Reykjavík 3c* ✉ Between Kirkjustræti, Vallarstræti and Pósthússtræti 🍽 Cafés and restaurants (£–£££). Try a window seat in the Café Paris (➤ 112) for a great view of the square

Bernhöftstorfan

A cluster of some of Reykjavík's oldest surviving buildings provides a charming centre for the Icelandic Travel Market and tourist office and the Lækjarbrekka restaurant. Dating from the end of the 18th century, this is an appealing group of wooden houses with Lækjartorg square just below. To the right, down broad Lækjargata, is an imposing white building with a flagpole. This is Government House (Stjórnarraðið), built in 1765. Formerly a prison workhouse, it now provides offices for the Prime Minister. On the little hill beside it stands a dramatic statue of Ingólfur Arnarson, the First Settler, by Einar Jónsson (➤ 84). To the left, the old grammar school was the first of its kind in Iceland, and lists Nobel prize-winning author Halldór Laxness (➤ 11) among former pupils.

✚ *Reykjavík 3c* ✉ Icelandic Travel Market and Internet café ☎ 522 4979 🍴 Lækjarbrekka (➤ 114)

Elliðaárdalur

Iceland prides itself on its policies of clean energy sources and conservation, both of which come together very successfully in this green valley lined with trees to the east of the city centre. It's a great place to escape the traffic, with a network of footpaths and cycle tracks. Running through its heart is the sparkling and unpolluted Elliðaá, site of Iceland's first hydroelectric power station and one of the best rivers for salmon in the country – rightly a source of national pride. It's the focus of the traditional opening of the fishing season on 1 May, and you can see the salmon spawning in early August. Many Icelandic horses are stabled here.

✚ Reykjavík 8b (off map) 🖐 Free 🚍 5, 6, 15, 18, 19

Hallgrímskirkja

Best places to see, ➤ 40–41.

Höfn (Old Harbour)

You might expect to find Reykjavík's harbour along Hafnarstræti (Harbour Street), but through the 20th century the boundaries were pushed seawards and the land extended artificially to provide more space, first to Tryggvagata and now Geirsgata. You can enjoy a stroll here and watch the fishing boats offloading in the western end, and perhaps admire a cruise liner or two in the eastern end. The new maritime museum, **Víkin,** is worth a look, and there's a good fish restaurant close by. Don't miss

the weekend fleamarket, **Kolaportið,** in the old Tollhús building with its beautiful mosaic wall on Tryggvagata. The market is full of bric-a-brac and clothing, with an excellent little food section selling fish and local delicacies.

➕ *Reykjavík 3b* 🚌 2, 3, 4, 5, 6, 7, 110, 112, 115 ❓ Annual Festival of the Sea celebrated in the old harbour

Víkin

✉️ Grandagarður 8 ☎️ 517 9400 🕐 Jun–Sep Tue–Sun 11–5; Oct–May Tue–Sun 1–5 ✋ Inexpensive 🚌 14

Kolaportið

✉️ Tryggvagata 19 ☎️ 562 5030 🕐 Sat–Sun 11–5
🍴 Café great for coffee and sandwiches (£)

Kjarvalsstaðir (Kjarval Collection)

The art gallery in Miklatún Park is primarily home to a collection of surreal landscapes by Iceland's most famous artist, Jóhannes S Kjarval (1885–1972). Kjarval began his working life as a trawlerman, but his skills as a painter were quickly recognized by his colleagues, who together raised the funds necessary for his study abroad, in London and Copenhagen. Stand back a little from the paintings for the best effect.
www.listafnreykjuvikur.is

✚ *Reykjavík 5e* ✉ Flókagata ☎ 552 6131
🕐 Daily 10–5 💲 Free 🍴 Café 🚌 11, 13
❓ Part of Reykjavík Art Museum

Laugardalur

Within walking distance of downtown Reykjavík, this is the city's main sports and recreation ground and it buzzes with families at weekends. The football stadium is here, as well as a fabulous outdoor **swimming pool** complete with waterslide, whirlpool and 'hot-pots' (geothermally heated, of course).

For children, there's all the fun of the Norse and Viking-themed Family Park and

Zoo (▶ 63), where you can stroke Icelandic horses and encounter other friendly beasts, including seals and reindeer. This is also the home of the **botanic gardens,** proof that Iceland's short growing season, unfriendly climate and volcanic soil are no obstacle to a wide range of plants and trees. Enjoy a picnic in the elegant heated pavilion. **Lauger Health and Spa Resort,** on Sundlaugavegur, is the biggest in Europe.

✚ *Reykjavík 8d* 🚌 2, 15, 17, 19
Swimming pool
🕐 Mon–Fri 6:30am–8:30pm, Sat–Sun 8am–10pm

Botanic gardens
🕐 Greenhouse and pavilion: Apr–Sep 10–10; Oct–Mar 10–5
🎟 Free 🍴 Café Flora
Lauger Health and Spa Resort
☎ 510 4500; www.spacity.is
🕐 Mon–Fri 6am–11:30pm, Sat 8am–10pm, Sun 8–8 🚌 14

Listasafn Íslands (National Gallery)

This tall white building with its high arched-eyebrow windows overlooks the Tjörn (➤ 88) and was originally a storage place for ice, cut from the pond and kept for use in the preservation of fish. It has been renovated in a light and modern style with lots of glass and woodblock floors to house the national collection of paintings and sculpture, which mostly date from the 20th century and include works by artists such as Nina Tryggvadóttir. It's not the biggest gallery, but the exhibitions change regularly.
www.listasafn.is

✚ *Reykjavík 3d* ✉ Fríkirkjuvegur 7 ☎ 515 9600 🕐 May–Sep Tue–Sun 10–5; Oct–Apr Tue–Sun 11–5 🎟 Free 🍴 Café (£)

a walk in the town centre/shore

From the statue of Leif the Lucky (▶ 11), in front of the Hallgrímskirkja, head down Skólavörðustígur.

This is an interesting street with lots of intriguing shops, galleries and jewellers, as well as the little stone gaol.

Bear right down Klapparstíggur, and turn right at the bottom onto Laugavegur.

This is Reykjavík's main shopping street, full of boutiques and, increasingly, bars.

Turn left onto Frakkastígur, with views up to the Hallgrímskirkja and down to the steel Viking ship sculpture, Sólfar, by Jón Gunnar Árnason (1931–89). At the bottom of the hill cross the busy road and turn left to follow the harbour path.

There are great views across the bay and to Mount Esja, with the harbour ahead.

Keep right past the harpoon-head sculpture and continue, with the fishing harbour opening out on your right to the sculpture of two fishermen. Turn right here and continue along the harbour, then bear left into Tryggvagata, which hooks you back towards the town centre. Turn right into the square, passing the Tourist Information Centre (toilets up to your right are free).

There are lots of bars and restaurants around this popular downtown area.

Keep right and turn up Aðalstræti, passing some of the city's oldest houses on your right. Number 10 is now a museum showing the growth of Reykjavík since 1786 (free). Pass the old well and pump, and turn left across a paved square to enter Austurvöllur square. Pass the old parliament building on your right, and go straight on, to turn left onto Lækjargata towards the harbour. Turn right up Bankastræti, and bear diagonally right up Skólavörðustígur to return to the Hallgrímskirkja.

Distance 3km (2 miles)
Time Allow at least half a day, longer to explore properly
Start/end point Hallgrímskirkja ✚ *Reykjavík 4d*
Lunch Café Sólon (➤ 113)

Listasafn Einars Jónssonar (Einar Jónsson Sculpture Museum)

High on the top of Skólavörðuholt hill, Iceland's outstanding sculptor Einar Jónsson (1874–1954) built a fortress-like house and gallery. The outside may be forbidding, but inside is a collection of fantastical sculpted figures which demonstrate the extraordinary imagination of the artist. Mythical creatures of gigantic proportions emerge from the living rocks of the Icelandic landscape, or swoop up from the seas in breathtaking beauty. Look out for the terrifying troll figure, petrified in the sunrise, the teeth in his skull-like face already becoming basalt columns; and the famous *Outlaws* statue, inspiration for one of Halldór Laxness's oddest heroes, Bjartur of Summerhouses. There are more sculptures in the garden. The artist's living quarters are at the top of narrow spiral stairs. **www.**skulptur.is

➕ *Reykjavík 4d* ✉ Eiríksgata ☎ 551 3797 🕐 Jun–Sep Tue–Sun 2–5; Sep–Nov, Feb–May Sat–Sun 2–5. Closed Dec–Jan 💷 Inexpensive ❓ Labels in Icelandic only; ask at the ticket desk for an invaluable sheet of translations

Öskjuhlíð

A massive space-age edifice, designed by architect Ingimundur Sveinsson, squats on Öskjuhlíð hill, to the south of town. Its great towers hold 18 million litres (3.9 million gallons) of geothermally heated water – enough to service half the city. Between them is an exhibition space on different levels, with a café, and a mini-geyser, which shoots up from the basement. The jewel in this crown is definitely on the top, however – the reflective glass dome is actually one of Reykjavík's most exclusive dining palaces, Perlan – The Pearl. The restaurant rotates as you eat – one complete

revolution takes two hours. Food with a view comes at a price, but you can go out on the balconies for free and see across to Mount Esja. The **Saga Museum** in one of the towers presents the history of Viking settlement in Iceland.

➕ *Reykjavík 5f* ✉ Perlan, Öskjuhlíð
☎ 562 0200 ⏰ Daily 🖐 Free 🍴 Café (£); Perlan restaurant (➤ 114) 🚌 18

Saga Museum
☎ 511 1517; www.sagamuseum.is

Þjóðmenning (Culture House)

Iceland is unique in having a written culture that goes back to its earliest days. The language, akin to Old Norse, has hardly changed over the last 1,000 years, and so the literature can be read as easily by people today as when it was written. The Sagas, complex and lively medieval tales of history, landscape, lineage and epic deeds, are still very much alive and at the heart of Icelandic culture, and this is the best place to learn more of their story. The sagas and other books were originally copied out on vellum, or calf skin. One calf skin would make just two pages, and many manuscripts ran to 200 pages and more. The manuscripts survive in books and fragments, gathered up by one man, Árni Magnússon, between 1702 and 1712. They were transported to Denmark for study, but unfortunately many were destroyed in the Great Fire of Copenhagen in 1728. The best were rescued, however, and in 1971 the first of these were returned to their homeland, including *Landnámabók*, *Íslandingabók* and *Njál's Saga*. Look out for the tiny wood-bound *Margaret's Saga*.

www.thjodmenning.is

✚ *Reykjavík 4c* ✉ Hverfisgata 15 ☎ 545 1400 🕐 Daily 11–5
🖐 Inexpensive; free Wed 🍴 Cafe (£) ❓ Temporary exhibitions on top floor

Þjóðminjasafn Íslands (National Museum)

This is the country's treasure house, fully refurbished in 2004 and an outstanding presentation. The Making of a Nation imaginatively displays Icelandic history and culture from the arrival of the first Viking settlers by boat, its scale inlaid in the wooden floor. Labelling and interactivity in English are excellent, culminating in an amusing array of 20th-century items presented on a slowly circulating airport carousel – to indicate modern Iceland's gateway to the world.

www.natmus.is

✚ *Reykjavík 2d* ✉ Suðurgata 41 ☎ 530 2200 🕐 May to mid-Sep daily 10–5; mid-Sep to Apr Tue–Sun 11–5 🖐 Inexpensive; free Wed 🍴 Café 🚌 12

Tjörnin

Of all Reykjavik's open spaces the area around the Tjörnin, or pond, is one of the most fun. Some 40 species of birds breed here, despite its city-centre location; the sound of ducks, geese and swans waiting to be fed will lead you straight to it. A walkway runs below the main road (Fríkirkjuvegur), offering good views of the old houses opposite. The big grey building at the northern end is the controversial City Hall – inside there's a tourist information desk and an exhibition area used mainly for photography and art. Locals say the best view of the lake is from the coffee shop, because you can't see the ugly modern lines of the City Hall itself.

✚ *Reykjavík 3d* ✉ Tourist Information, City Hall ☎ 411 1005 ④ Mon–Fri 8:20–4:30, Sat noon–4pm; also Sun noon–4pm May–Sep ✋ Free 🍴 Café in City Hall (£)

Viðey

The citizens of Reykjavík come to this romantic island to get away from it all. Low-lying and green, it's ten minutes off shore and easily explored in a day. The Imagine Peace Tower, a strong beam of light, illuminates the sky here in winter and is visible for miles. It is a memorial to John Lennon by Yoko Ono, and a beacon for world peace.

There was once a monastery here and the island is full of history. Around 1755, entrepreneur and Royal Superintendent Skúli Magnússon had a stone house built as a sign of wealth and confidence (the oldest original building in Iceland, now restored to hold the restaurant). His attempts to turn the fortunes of Reykjavík failed and he died bankrupt in 1794 – there's a memorial to him by the church. A small community made the island their home in the last century, centring their hopes on a fishery, but it too failed and now the village is deserted.

www.videy.com

✚ 18K ✉ Kollafjörður 🍴 Viðeyjarstofa ☎ 562 1934: afternoon coffee and cake ⛴ Ferry from Sundahöfn or Midbakki ☎ 533 5055 for information and booking ❓ Peace Tower illuminated 9 Oct–8 Dec

Ylströndin Nauthólsvík

Golden sands and coastal swimming are not what you expect to find in Iceland. But here, in the shadow of Reykjavík airport, a facility offering just that opened in 2000. The sand comes from Skaftafell and the water is geothermally heated to 19–20°C (66–68°F) in the lagoon.

✚ *Reykjavík 4f (off map)* ✉ South of Öskjuhlíð ☎ 511 6630; www.itr.is
🕐 May–Sep 10–8 🥤 Free, but small charge for use of changing rooms

More to see in the West

ARNARSTAPI

The delightful cove of Arnarstapi is perfectly set on the end of the great Snæfellsnes peninsula, its steep cliffs and stacks home to a myriad screaming sea birds, its wooden holiday cottages all turned to face the view and the sunshine. As you turn down towards the sheltered harbour, you can't miss the gigantic boulderous, be-hatted figure on the clifftop to your right. He's Bárður Snæfellsás, a spirit who lives in the great mountain of Snæfellsjökull, which shelters the village to the north. The cliffs are riddled with blowholes and echoing caves and, to the west, there's a natural stone arch. The coastline is a nature reserve, and from the car park above the harbour you can take the footpath to neighbouring Hellnar.

A small community of New Age enthusiasts live here, attracted by the supposed magic properties of the mountain. **www**.ust.is

🕇 2F 🖾 On the southwest end of Snæfellsnes peninsula, Route 574 🍴 Snjófell restaurant at Arnarstapi (£–££); café and hotel at Hellnar (££–£££) 🚢 Boat trips and whale-watching from Ólafsvík, contact Seatours ☎ 433 2254; www.seatours.is ❓ For cycle hire, snowmobiling and camping contact Snjófell, Arnarstapi ☎ 435 6783; www.snjofell.is

BLÁA LÓNIÐ (BLUE LAGOON)

Best places to see, ➤ 34–35.

BORGARNES

Travelling northwards on Route 1 you turn a corner to see the pretty town of Borgarnes stretched out along its narrow peninsula on the opposite shore of Borgarfjörður. In its beautiful but exposed location, with the plains of Myrar behind and the mountains to the west and south, it catches all the available light and sunshine. This is Iceland's biggest non-fishing town. A little white church with a dark-hatted steeple dominates the skyline, giving it an unexpectedly Alpine air. There are strong connections in this area with *Egil's Saga*, and Egil's father Skallagrímur was buried in the town's triangle of green park, with his horse and other accoutrements as befitted a great chief. The relief depicts Egil himself, carrying the body of his son Böðvar, who drowned near by. The new **Settlement Centre** offers an outstanding interpretation of tales from *Egil's Saga*, and a second exhibition on the settlement of Iceland.

✚ 18J ☒ On Route 1, 74km (46 miles) north of Reykjavík 🚌 All Reykjavík buses pass through on their way to the West Fjords or Akureyri

ℹ Tourist Information Centre at Bruartorg

☎ 437 2214; www.west.is

Settlement Centre

☒ Brákarbraut 13–15 ☎ 437 1600 🖐 Daily 🍴 Café

BÚÐARDALUR

This unassuming farming community at the head of
Hvammsfjörður marks the gateway to Laxárdalur –
the salmon river valley and setting for Iceland's
most romantic *Laxdæla Saga*. The tale is set around
the tragic love of two foster brothers, Kjartan and
Bolli, for the lovely Guðrun Ósvífursdóttir. A replica
Viking longhouse has been built at **Eiríksstaðir,**
the birthplace of adventurer Leifur Eiríksson, and
in summer costumed staff bring his story to life.

➕ 5E ✉ On Route 60, 154km (95 miles) north of Reykjavík

Eiríksstaðir

☎ 434 1118; www.leif.is ⏱ Jun–Sep daily 9–6

✋ Inexpensive

FLATEY

Best places to see, ➤ 36–37.

GULLFOSS AND GEYSIR

Best places to see, ➤ 38–39.

HAFNARFJÖRÐUR

Overshadowed by neighbouring
Reykjavík, Hafnarfjörður has
always boasted a better natural
harbour and has been a busy
fishing port for over 60 years. It
hosts the Hafnarfjörður Museum,
but is perhaps best known locally
as the town which takes elves
seriously. So seriously, in fact, that roads have been diverted to
avoid upsetting the little people. Thanks to the work of a local seer,
there's now a 'Hidden World' map available at the tourist
information centre showing pixie hot-spots around the town.

Hafnarfjörður is also the centre for modern Viking activities, offering an imaginative Viking-themed restaurant, Fjöru Garðurinn, in a magnificent old wooden house down by the harbour in the **Viking Village.** This is the focus for the riotous activities of the June International Viking Festival (➤ 22–23), complete with a Viking 'street', and some pretty lively behaviour on Friday and Saturday nights too.

www.hafnarfjordur.is

✚ 18K 🍴 Full range of cafés and restaurants (£–£££) 🚢 Short and long sea trips available, including whale-watching and sea angling

🛈 Strandgata 6 ☎ 585 5500 ⏰ Daily 8–5; also Jul–Aug Sat–Sun 10–3

Viking Village

☎ 565 1213; www.vikingvillage.is

HAFNIR

The Reykjanes peninsula marks the southwestern end of the great geological fault which runs diagonally across the country. On its furthest tip is the scattered former fishing village of Hafnir. You can discover more about Iceland's piscatorial heritage at the fascinating **aquarium,** well stocked with local sea and freshwater fish. Look out for the anchor of the ghost ship *Jamestown*; abandoned off the coast of America in 1867, it drifted ashore here three years later, complete with its cargo of timber. To the south, the rocks swarm with migrant and nesting birds, including gannets from the offshore island of Eldey.

www.reykjanes.is

➕ 17K 🐋 Whale- and dolphin-spotting trips from Keflavík ☎ 421 7777
ℹ Hafnagata 57 ☎ 421 6777

Sæfiskasafnið (Aquarium)

☎ 421 6958 🕐 Jun–Aug daily 2–5:30; Sep–May daily 2–4
✋ Inexpensive

HEKLA

The country's most infamous – and still very active – volcano last erupted in March 2000, and Icelanders are holding their breath waiting for the big one. It is known to erupt about every ten years, with the last major eruption in 1991, but scientists suspect that recent rumblings may herald a new period of activity. The volcano forms a ridged mountain 1,491m (4,892ft) high on the great geological rift which divides Iceland, looming over the lowlands of the southwest with its top usually hidden modestly away in cloud. In the Middle Ages it was notorious throughout Europe as the gateway to hell. Visit the **Hekla Centre** and watch the audiovisual explanations to learn more.

➕ 21K

Hekla Centre

✉ By Hotel Leirubakki, on Route 26 ☎ 487 8700 🕐 All year (ring for opening times) ✋ Inexpensive

HELLISSANDUR

Set on the northwestern tip of the Snæfellsnes peninsula, on the edge of the black lava field that flows down from Snæfellsjökull, this town has spectacular views to the cliffs of the West Fjords. At the **Maritime Museum** you can explore an old fisherman's hut and boat, and there are lots of paths and tracks to follow amid the lava. Hellissandur's biggest claim to fame is the towering radio mast, 412m (1,351ft) high, which was the tallest structure in Europe when it was built in 1959. In such a windy place, the mast would have snapped off had it been dug into the ground, so instead it is balanced on a point and held up by wires.

✚ 2E ✉ On Route 574, 245km (152 miles) northwest of Reykjavík

Sjómannagarðurinn við Útnesveg (Maritime Museum)

✉ Útnesvegur ☎ 436 6619 ◷ Jun–Aug Tue–Sun 9:30–4
✋ Inexpensive

HORNSTRANDIR

Hornstrandir has always been remote and isolated; in the days when people lived on its fjords, the only way in or out was by sea, and it's the same today. Its high barren uplands, lush lowlands and rugged cliffs are protected now as a nature reserve, and the banning of sheep as well as vehicles has meant a return of the land to meadow and wild flowers. To reach this hiker's paradise, catch the boat from Ísafjörður, making sure you have everything you need with you for several days – there's no accommodation other than emergency huts and the odd summer house, and you must be prepared for every sort of weather. You'll be rewarded by peace and, with luck, an abundance of wildlife.

www.westfjords.is

✚ 5B ✉ Northern tip of West Fjords, access on foot or by boat only 🚢 Scenic boat trips and tours from Ísafjörður, by West Tours ☎ 456 5111; www.westtours.is

HÚSAFELL

This beautiful spot near the head of a long valley is covered in low birch trees and littered with gaily painted summer houses, testament to its warm temperatures and handy supply of natural hot water. A popular centre for camping, it is set about with attractive wilderness and ice caps, notably Eiríksjökull, Langjökull and Ok. You can take the high road over to Kaldidalur or hike from the valley head to explore the lava caves – the longest, Kalmanshellir, is 4km (2.5 miles).

www.husafell.is

🚩 20H ✉ On Route 518, east of Reykholt ☎ 435 1550 (accommodation) 🍴 Snack bar (£–££) 🚌 Daily bus in summer from Reykjavík via Þingvellir and Kaldidalur ❓ Guided walks to the caves ☎ 435 1558

from Reykjavík to Húsafell

Explore small towns, a beautiful long valley and a spectacular fjord.

Take Route 1 north from Reykjavík, via Mosfellsbær. At Hvalfjörður follow signs for the tunnel (toll payable). At the other side, turn left onto Route 51 to Akranes. Turn off before Akranes on the 503 for the Akranes Museum (▶ 100). Head north on Route 51. Turn left and left again, and follow Route 1 to Borgarnes (▶ 91).

To the left, the fertile plains are dotted with farms; to your right are sweeping fells of black scree, giving way to bushy vegetation.

Cross the causeway to Borgarnes and on Route 1 stay towards Akureyri.

This beautiful wide valley is a popular holiday spot, with marked walking trails, and a great viewpoint at Svignaskarð.

Turn right at the octagonal service station, Baulan, on Route 50 to Reykholt. Stay on this road, signed to Reykholt, then bear left towards Reykholt on the 518 after 5km (3 miles).

Explore the church, museum centre and Snorri's pool (► 104). The Fosshótel Reykholt is just behind.

Continue on Route 518 to Húsafell (► 97), passing the lovely Hraunfossar waterfalls on your left. Stay on the 518 around the head of the valley. At Brúará bridge, stay on the 523 to pass a café at Bjarnastaðir; at the junction with the 522 turn left, and right onto Route 50 to Borgarnes. Turn left onto Route 1 and retrace route south to the junction with Route 47. Turn left here for Hvalfjörður (► 100) and take the old road around this fabulous fjord. Rejoin Route 1 and return to Reykjavík.

Distance 300km (186 miles)
Time Allow a full day, or take it slowly over two days
Start/end point A circular route from Reykjavík ✚ 18K
Lunch Fosshótel Reykholt (££)

HVALFJÖRÐUR

It is said that you may see up to 17 species of whale in this deep fjord during late summer. The whales were particularly welcomed in days gone by – you can see something of the history of local whaling (which stopped in 1989 and then resumed in 2003) and the 'Cod Wars' at the excellent **Akranes Museum.** This narrow finger of water is sheltered by Mount Esja to the south and Skarðsheiði to the north and, now that it has been bypassed by the tunnel at Saurbær, it has returned to something like tranquillity, with only the ferro-silicon smelter on the northern shore to mar its beauty. Irish monks were the first settlers here, commemorated by a stone in the cemetery at Akranes. It's difficult to imagine this peaceful place bristling with naval hardware, but during World War II the Allies had a massive base here and it was a key location for the North Atlantic convoys.

➕ 18J ✉ 43km (27 miles) north of Reykjavík

Akranes Museum

✉ Garður, by Akranes ☎ 431 5566; www.museum.is ⏰ May–Sep daily 10–6; Sep–Apr daily 1–6 💰 Moderate 🍴 Café in the Museum Hall

HVERAGERÐI

You'll notice that there are no tower blocks in this town – it's built on the edge of an active geothermal area and small earthquakes are commonplace. Steam from the naturally hot water (reaching 200°C/392°F underground) is used to heat greenhouses – pause at Eden on Austurmörk for souvenirs and a taste of tropical plantlife. There's good walking in the hills, and a geothermal area in the town centre with boiling mud pots and sulphurous fumaroles. You could even treat yourself to a mudbath at the health spa. One spring is named Ruslahver, or 'garbage hot spring', after the rubbish that had been tipped down it when it was a dry hole resurfaced during an earthquake.

➕ 19K ✉ On Route 1, 38km (24 miles) southeast of Reykjavík 🍴 Café with pastries to die for at Hverabakarí (bakery), Breiðamörk 10 ☎ 483 4879
ℹ Sunnumörk 2–4 ☎ 483 4601; www.south.is

HVOLSVÖLLUR

In the flat, fertile land north of the Thverá River lies the village of Hvolsvöllur, all too easily bypassed by the hurrying tourist anxious for the next great sight. Instead, pause awhile, for you are entering the magical country of one of the greatest of epics, *Njál's Saga*, and the **Saga Centre** here will help you to make sense of it all. As

well as exhibitions explaining the characters, the story and its locations, the centre sets this best-loved Saga in the context of the Viking age. Storytelling was once a fundamental part of Icelandic life and is revived here in a specially recreated medieval hall.

➕ 20L ✉ 106km (66 miles) southeast of Reykjavík
Sögusetrið (Saga Centre)
✉ Hlíðarvegur 16 ☎ 487 8781; www.njala.is 🕐 May–Sep daily 9–7 💰 Inexpensive 🍴 Hlíðarendi restaurant (£–££) ❓ Musical presentation in various languages Jul–Aug 7pm; booking essential

ÍSAFJÖRÐUR

Dramatically set on a narrow spit in an inlet of the wide Ísafjarðarjúp fjord and sheltered by steep mountains, Ísafjörður is the capital of the remote and beautiful West Fjords region. It is the jumping-off point for a wide range of activities including mini-cruises, whale-watching, hiking and sea angling in summer, and skiing in winter, and is also the gateway to Hornstrandir (► 96). The town was one of Iceland's key trading ports from 1569 to the early 19th century, and a complex of four old wooden houses on the harbour, now a maritime museum, bears testament to this. Cod, shark and herring were all sought with *Þilskip (thilskip)* – small boats with decks – instead of the more common open rowing boats.

www.vestfirdir.is

🞤 3B ✉ 457km (283 miles) north of Reykjavík

❓ Boat trips to Hornstrandir and Vigur island, daily in summer

ℹ Aðalstræti 7 ☎ 450 8060

🕐 Mon–Fri 8–6, and summer weekends 10–3

KRÝSUVÍK

Iceland has around 200 volcanoes and 250 natural hot springs, and has produced about one third of the total world lava flow in the last 400 years. If you've only got a short time to visit Iceland, then this is the most interesting geothermal site near Reykjavík where you can stroll among smelly steam holes and horribly bubbling mud pools – it's no surprise to learn that sulphur was once mined here. The gloriously multicoloured volcanic scoria beneath your feet can be hot and uncertain, so be careful where you tread and stick to the boardwalks. The whole area is part of the Reykjanesfólkvangur national reserve.

✚ 18L ✉ South of Reykjavík on Route 42

LÁTRABJARG

Nowhere in Iceland are the seabirds so tightly packed along the cliffs as here, on the western-most point of Europe. This older rock, in a sheer, undulating line of cliffs that stretch some 11km (7 miles) and rise to 511m (1,676ft) high, has been worn and ground on its exposed seaward surface to form natural ledges, which are like high-rise penthouses to a vast density of kittiwakes and fulmars, guillemots, puffins and one-third of the world's total population of razorbills. From a distance it is like watching a swarming beehive as the birds fly up and down and out to sea, and close up the noise of their calling is incredible. In days gone by, hardy locals would lower themselves over the edge on a rope to collect the eggs in a test of bravery, skill and basic survival.

✚ 1D ✉ Western tip of the West Fjords

REYKHOLT

The greatest of Icelandic writers Snorri Sturluson (➤ 11) lived in this beautiful rolling valley from 1206 to 1241, composing his mighty history of Norwegian kings, *Heimskringla*. He had his own thermal bathing pool, Snorralaug, once linked straight to his farm by a tunnel, which you can see steaming beyond the church. The **Modern Centre for Medieval Research** is dedicated to him – with its tall-hatted spire, it's a distinctive landmark. A statue of Snorri stands outside the former grammar school, now home to the National Library.

✚ 19H ✉ Turn left off Route 527, in the Hvíta valley, 43km (27 miles) east of Borgarnes

🛈 Reykholtskirkju ☎ 433 8000

Snorrastofa-Heimskringla (Modern Centre for Medieval Research)
✉ 320 Reykholt ☎ 435 1490; www.snorrastofa.is ⏱ May–Sep daily 10–6; Oct–Apr Mon–Fri 10–5 🍴 Fosshótel Reykholt behind old farmstead ☎ 435 1260 ❓ Car parks below centre and futher along main road; centre is focus of an annual music festival in July

SKÁLHOLT

The stark white **church** at Skálholt stands out of the green landscape like a beacon. It is only 50 years old but there have been similar buildings on this important site for centuries since one of the country's first two bishoprics was founded here in 1056. In 1550 the community was taught a sharp lesson when rebel

Catholic bishop Jón Arason was summarily beheaded for opposing the introduction of Lutheranism from Denmark. Skálholt remained a (now Lutheran) bishopric until a general migration to Reykjavík at the end of the 18th century. In the church you can admire the massive stone sarcophagus of another early bishop, Páll Jónsson, and the striking modern mosaic of Christ by artist Nina Tryggvadóttir. Archaeological excavations around the church are revealing the scale of the original farming settlement.

✚ 20K ✉ Northeast of Selfoss on Route 31, just north of Laugarás

Church

✉ Biskupstungur, 801 Selfoss ☎ 486 8860 ⓒ Daily 🍴 Café in school ❓ Free concerts at weekends in Jul and Aug

SNÆFELLSJÖKULL

On a clear day you can see the iced pixie-hat peak of this mountain, apparently floating weightlessly above the sea, all the way from Reykjavík. It's not the biggest glacier in the country, but one of the most appealing and accessible. Perched on the end of the long ridge of Snæfellsnes, the views from the top are fantastic. Jules Verne picked it as the gateway to the underworld in *Journey to the Centre of the Earth* (he obviously hadn't been through the 6.4km/ 4-mile Hvalfjördur tunnel), and even today it revels in a dubious mystical reputation, which acts as a magnet for New Agers and free spirits. You can get to the top fairly easily from Arnarstapi or Ólafsvík by snowmobile or skidoo – make sure you stick to your guide's tracks in summer, when crevasses can be dangerous. It's a popular spot for family picnics and tobogganing.

www.ust.is; www.snaefellsnes.com

✚ 2F ✉ Western tip of Snæfellsnes, 195km (121 miles) northwest of Reykjavík ❓ Glacier trips from Arnarstapi (➤ 90) and Ólafsvík

ℹ Snæfellsjökull National Park Visitor Centre, Hellnar ☎ 436 6888

STYKKISHÓLMUR

This windblown town on the north shore of Snæfellsnes is an odd mixture of good, bad and plain ugly. Approaching by road, you see the sweeping white pylon 'H' of the church off to your right, a lively and daring piece of modern architecture. There are some splendid old wooden houses down by the harbour, including the black-painted Norwegian House of 1832, now a museum and gallery but built as the home of Iceland's first meteorologist, Árni Thorlacius. The old centre is dominated by the looming ochre walls of a Franciscan convent, however, which seems out of place amid the gaily painted houses. Paganism has always had a place here and to prove it there's a magical hill, Helgafell, where – if you follow the rules – you may be granted three wishes. Look out for scallop shells in the bay; the other local speciality is traditionally cured shark (*hákarl*) – follow your nose westwards to Bjarnarhöfn.

www.stykkisolmur.is

🚌 3E ✉ At the end of Route 58 🍴 Several restaurants and snack bars ⛴ Ferry sailings and wildlife tours, Seatours ☎ 438 1454; www.seatours.is ❓ Baldur, the car and passenger ferry across Breiðafjörður bay to Flatey and the West Fjords, leaves here on its daily circuit

ℹ Borgarbraut ☎ 438 1750 🕐 Summer: daily 7am–10pm; winter: Sat–Sun 10–7

ÞINGVELLIR (THINGVELLIR)

Best places to see, ▶ 50–51.

ÞÓRSMÖRK (THORSMORK)

One of the world's great treks, from the extraordinary lunarscape of Landmannalaugar (▶ 150), leads over the mountains to this remote and beautiful nature reserve set about with birch woods, entwined rivers and superb glacier-topped scenery. It's a wilderness with its own warmer microclimate, best explored on foot. Don't expect to drive there unless you're with an experienced group – the road into the valley crosses the powerful and dangerous Krossá River, and this is best left to the experts with their specially high-set coaches.

✚ 21L ✉ Access up F249, off Route 1 south of Hvolsvöllur

VESTMANNAEYJAR (WESTMANN ISLANDS)

Best places to see, ▶ 52–53.

HOTELS

REYKJAVÍK

Baldursbrá (£–££)

Friendly guest house offering comfortable and spacious bed and breakfast accommodation in a quiet quarter within a few minutes' walk of the town centre. Proprietor Evelyne is a source of local knowledge. A free shuttle service links to the Flybus airport connection.

✉ Laufásvegur 41 ☎ 552 6646 🕐 All year

Hóll Cottage (£££)

This lovely historic cottage on a side street in the centre of town offers you a quiet space to call your own within easy walking distance of all the main attractions. Beautifully restored and thoughtfully equipped, sleeps 4–6, self-catering.

✉ Grjótagata 12 ☎ 864 4481; www.simnet.is/holl 🕐 All year

Hótel Borg (£££)

Iceland's oldest and smartest hotel, restored to 1930s art deco splendour, and complete with ballroom. Every bedroom is decorated with a different theme. A new top floor was added in 2006.

✉ Pósthússtræti 11 ☎ 551 1440; www.hotelborg.is 🕐 All year

Hótel Holt (£££)

A stylish and luxurious modern hotel set discreetly amid the international embassies in a gracious part of the town centre. Boasts a fine restaurant, as well as modern art on every wall.

✉ Bergstaðastræti 37 ☎ 552 5700; www.holt.is 🕐 All year

BORGARNES

Bjarg (£–££)

Comfortable bed and breakfast accommodation in a splendid old gabled farmhouse outside the town; good walking in the area.

✉ By Borgarnes ☎ 437 1925; www.farmholidays.is 🕐 All year

LÁTRABJARG
Breiðavík (£–££)
Simple bed and breakfast accommodation in a renovated former schoolhouse. Convenient for exploring the bird cliffs, and offers fishing permits for the local lakes.

✉ Látrabjarg ☎ 456 1575; www.breidavik.net 🕙 May–Sep

SNÆFELLSNES
Guesthouse Langaholt (£–££)
You're guaranteed a friendly welcome at this family hotel, in a fantastic setting on a long sandy beach with its own 9-hole golf course and views to the Snæfell glacier. Variety of rooms and facilities available, from sleeping-bag up to a high standard of comfort with your own bathroom.

✉ Garðar ☎ 435 6789; www.langaholt.is 🕙 Mar–Nov

Hótel Hellnar (££–£££)
This pleasant, timber-clad hotel has been certified for its policy of sustainable ecotourism since 2002, and offers glacier tours and horse-riding as well as fabulous views over the coastline. Next door to the National Park Visitor Centre.

✉ Brekkubær, Hellnar ☎ 435 6820; www.hellnar.is 🕙 May–Sep, other times by arrangement

RESTAURANTS

REYKJAVÍK
Á Næstu Grösum (£)
Excellent downtown vegetarian restaurant, with buffet-style section, home-made bread and cakes and organic wines.

✉ Laugavegur 20b ☎ 552 8410; www.anaestugrosum.is 🕙 Mon–Sat lunch and dinner, Sun dinner only

Café Paris (£)
The green building on the corner of Austervöllur square – get yourself a window table and watch the world go by. Can be very busy. Pancakes with ice cream are especially good.

✉ Austervöllur ☎ 551 1020 🕙 Lunch and dinner

Café Sólon (£)

Wooden chairs, candles and art on the walls give this corner restaurant a cosmopolitan air, and it's perfectly set for a lunchtime break when you've been shopping 'til you're dropping on Laugavegur. Sample the bread and tapenade, or perhaps the seafood soup, and leave room for the cake of the day. Good vegetarian choices too.

✉ Bankastræti 7A ☎ 562 3232 ⏱ Lunch and dinner

The Deli (£)

For food on the run, don't miss this little snack bar at the bottom of Skolavörðustígur. Look through to the kitchen to see your food being freshly prepared with top-quality ingredients – pasta salads, paninis with sundried tomatoes and mozzarella, focaccia, pizzas and tasty sandwiches. Also at the University, beside the National Museum.

✉ Bankastræti 14 ☎ 551 6000; www.deli.is ⏱ 10–6

Einar Ben (££–£££)

Set in the upper part of an elegant old red town house, above a woollen goods shop, this stylish restaurant and bar is close to the main tourist information centre. Try langoustine tails with salt cod cannelloni, or flounder fillets in a parsley crust, followed by white chocolate cheesecake with wild strawberry ice cream.

✉ Veltusund 1 ☎ 511 5090; www.einarben.is ⏱ Dinner

EldSmiðjan (£)

Wonderful smells waft from the wood-fired oven as you enter this corner-set pizza house, just down from the Hallgrímskirkja. It's good, simple food at its best. Downstairs is a busy takeaway and upstairs it's cosy, with room for just a few to sit. The menus come in all the varieties you'd expect, but with some interesting variations. Try a fiery Hekla; and an *ostagerðarmannsins* (old cheesemaker) comes with mozarella, cream cheese, parmesan and blue cheese.

✉ Bragagötu 38A ☎ 562 3838 ⏱ Lunch and dinner

Fylgifiskar (£–££)

Enjoy soup and a choice of three hot dishes at this remarkable seafish emporium, overlooking Laugardalur. Owner Guðbörg Glóð Logadottír has studied all aspects of fish preparation, and serves over 30 different kinds, all fresh and flavoursome, delicately spiced. You can also buy it ready prepared to cook yourself. Sesam Bleikja – Arctic char with sesame, coriander and chilli – is a speciality. There's a branch at Skólavörðustígur 8 (➤ 57).

✉ Suðurlandsbraut 10 ☎ 533 1300 ⏰ Lunch Mon–Fri, and Sat in winter

Lækjarbrekka (££–£££)

The old wooden house is one of Reykjavík's most popular restaurants, famous for its traditional dishes including mountain lamb and a summer lobster feast. The atmosphere is cosy behind the lace curtains, and the food is delicious.

✉ Bankastræti 2 ☎ 551 4430 ⏰ Lunch and dinner, and afternoon café

Perlan (£££)

Gives a whole new meaning to the term 'top restaurant', built in a revolving glass dome on the city's hot-water tanks. Dining is formal but excellent – locals come here for an expensive treat.

✉ Öskjuhlið ☎ 562 0200; www.perlan.is ⏰ Dinner daily

Restaurant Hornið (£–££)

An old golden-painted restaurant and bar high on a corner near the post office, serving a wide range of fresh seafood, pizzas and pasta. The food is terrific and affordable.

✉ Hafnarstræti 15 ☎ 551 3340 ⏰ Lunch and dinner

Sjávarbarinn (£–££)

You won't find much fresher than the fish at this restaurant in a terrace row by the harbour, near the Maritime Museum. The lunchtime buffet bar offers good value, or try the fish and chips, Icelandic style.

✉ Grandagardi 9 ☎ 517 3131; www.sjavarbarinn.com ⏰ Mon–Sat lunch and dinner, Sun dinner only

Sjávarkjallarinn (££–£££)

One of Reykjavík's trendiest restaurants, in a stone-built cellar beneath the main tourist office. Fish dishes are prepared with oriental overtones, but meat-eaters and vegetarians are also well catered for.

✉ Adalstræti 2 ☎ 511 1212 🕔 Mon–Sat lunch and dinner, Sun dinner only

Svarta Kaffið (£–££)

Upstairs bar and coffee house on Laugavegur with an unusual but very tasty lunchtime speciality – *súpa í brauði* – which is home-made soup served *in* a crusty bread roll. Light meals available.

✉ Laugavegur 54 ☎ 551 2999 🕔 Lunch and dinner

Tapas Barinn (££)

Spanish tapas with an Icelandic twist is the theme at this popular new restaurant. Try tasty morsels of Icelandic lamb, seafood and puffin served tapas-style, with the fragrance of olive oil and garlic.

✉ Vesturgata 3b ☎ 551 2344; www.tapas.is 🕔 Dinner only

Þrír (Thrír) Frakkar (££–£££)

A curious restaurant with a popular reputation for fish, and an owner with a distinctive sense of humour – the name can mean three Frenchmen or three overcoats, and he chose the latter. Decor has an off-beat kitsch feel – note the dried fish clock on the wall. You can taste a traditional Icelandic dish of combined fish and potato *(plokkfiskur)*, served with black bread. Other fish dishes tend to be served with strong, creamy sauces. Soup of the day is included in the price. Whale meat is a speciality.

✉ Baldursgata 14 ☎ 552 3939 🕔 Lunch Mon–Fri, dinner daily

Við Tjörnina (£££)

The best restaurant in town for fish is hidden between the Tjörn and the Lutheran cathedral on the first floor of an unprepossessing place. The decor includes old lace, pretty china and home-made menus. Marinaded cod-cheeks are the house speciality and taste infinitely better than they sound. Highly recommended.

✉ Templarasund 3 ☎ 551 8666 🕔 Dinner only

HAFNARFJÖRÐUR

Fjörukráin (£–££)

Magnificent Viking-themed restaurant and bar by the harbour. Bold, imaginative decor and an eccentric atmosphere.

✉ Strandgata 55 ☎ 565 1890; www.fjorkrain.is ◷ Lunch and dinner

ENTERTAINMENT

CINEMA

Reykjavík has several cinemas showing films in their original language with Icelandic subtitles.

✉ Sambió, Álfabakki 8 ☎ 587 8900 ✉ Sambió, Kringlan ☎ 575 8900
✉ Laugarásbíó, Laugarás ☎ 553 2075

LIVE ARTS

Iceland Opera

The national opera company boasts the northernmost opera house in the world. Limited performances in summer.

✉ Ingólfsstræti, Reykjavík ☎ 511 4200; www.opera.is

Iceland Symphony Orchestra

Offers world-class international programmes throughout the year. Its new permanent home will be the National Concert Hall in the East Harbour from 2009.

✉ Háskólabíó, Reykjavík ☎ 545 2500; www.sinfonia.is

National Theatre

Quality drama. Shakespeare performed in Icelandic.

✉ Hverfisgata 19, Reykjavík ☎ 551 1200

Reykjavík City Theatre

Lively dance, theatre and musicals, as well as touring productions.

✉ Listabraut 3, Reykjavík ☎ 588 0900

Salurinn, Kópavogur

Iceland's first purpose-built concert hall hosts a wide range of music, from chamber music to jazz.

✉ Hamraborg 6, Kópavogur ☎ 570 0400; www.salurinn.is

The North and Northeast

Akureyri

The north coast is characterized by some of the most beautiful fjordland scenery, with sweeping vistas of high mountains and fertile green valleys.

The area offers some of the country's best salmon fishing, whale-spotting and birdlife, as well as the most spectacular geothermal area around Mývatn and more than its fair share of magnificent waterfalls.

The eastern part is bleaker, with rolling brown moorland, and marshland on the northern tip. In summer there is good access to the vast empty spaces of the interior, lit up by the occasional welcome oasis of green.

AKUREYRI

Despite its location so close to the Arctic Circle, Iceland's northern capital has the reputation of a banana belt. It may get more snow and cold weather in winter than Reykjavík, but this is more than compensated for by greater warmth and sunshine in summer. Locals make the most of this by growing trees and flowers everywhere – in tubs, window boxes and gardens – and it's known as a floral town. Artists also flourish here.

Agriculturally, this is one of the richest areas in Iceland and you'll see lots of red-roofed farms dotted along the shores of Eyjafjörður. Farmers first settled here in Viking times, when it became known as a trading area. However, the town itself only developed in the late 18th century, in two distinct halves – the old Danish town around Aðalstræti and the Icelandic town around the modern harbour. They met in the middle with the theatre in 1902, where you can still see the old harbour walls. Akureyri now boasts a population of 17,000 and its own university.

You can easily walk around the pleasant old centre in a day. There are good shops and eating places, an interesting church, a lovely botanic garden and numerous little museums to explore. Einar Jónsson's famous *Outlaws* statue stands on Eyarlandsvegur near the park. A stroll past the old houses along Aðalstræti is a must. The town claims the world's most northerly 18-hole golf course, Jaðarsvöllur, and all are welcome at the Arctic Open tournament, held through the hours of midnight sun in June (► 22).

www.nordurland.is; www.visitakureyri.is

✚ 10C ✉ 389km (241 miles) northeast of Reykjavík on Route 1 🍴 Range of eating places (£–£££) 🚌 Daily coach service from Reykjavík ☎ 462 4442; scheduled air services from Reykjavík with Air Iceland ☎ 460 7000 ⛴ Regular ferry service to Hrísey and Grímsey ☎ 462 7733 ❓ Artic Open: www.arcticopen.is ℹ️ Bus terminal, Hafnarstræti 82 ☎ 553 5999; 🕐 Oct–May Mon–Fri 8–4; Jun–Aug Mon–Fri 7:30–7, Sat–Sun 8–7; Sep Mon–Fri 8–5, Sat–Sun 8–noon

Akureyrarkirkja

In summer a steady stream of visitors makes its way up the long flight of steps from the corner of Hafnarstræti and Kaupvangsstræti to the white-painted church at the top. With its stumpy twin towers and square front it's not Iceland's most beautiful church, but it's interesting nevertheless as a forerunner of Reykjavík's Hallgrímskirkja (➤ 40–41); also designed by Guðjón Samúelsson, it was built in 1940. Inside, the stained glass shows important scenes from Icelandic history. The distinguished central window in the chancel is a survivor of the old Coventry Cathedral in England. Removed for safekeeping during World War II, it was eventually sold to an Icelander who presented it to the new church.

www.akirkja.is

☎ 462 7700 🕓 Jun–Aug daily 10–12, 2–5 🖐 Free ❓ Service 11am Sun

Kjarnaskógar

Carry on south of town towards the airport for a few kilometres and you'll reach this beautiful area of woodland, mainly birch and conifer, set on a sunny hillside. It's a favourite with local people at weekends – there are lots of walking trails and good places for picnics and barbecues.

✉ Just south of town on Route 821 🕓 Open access 🖐 Free

Minjasafn Akureyrar (Folk Museum)

The town's beautifully presented museum occupies a modern building screened by trees on Aðalstræti. Displays, including a rare ship burial on the the ground floor, bring the history of Iceland to life. The little church below it is part of the museum, moved to this location from Svalbarðseyri on the opposite shore.

✉ Aðalstræti 58 ☎ 462 4162; www.akmus.is ③ Jun–Sep daily 10–5;
Sep–May Sat 2–4 ✋ Inexpensive ❓ Summer concerts held in
the church

Nonnahús

You can pick out 'Nonni's House' on Aðalstræti from the life-sized
statue of a friendly looking fellow in hat and cloak, in the garden
of the pink house in front. Nonni was the nickname of Jesuit
priest Jón Sveinsson (1857–1944), a widely travelled man who
incorporated his own adventures into stories for children which
in turn became famous across Europe.

www.nonni.is

✉ Aðalstræti 54a ☎ 462 3555 ③ Jun–Aug daily 10–5 ✋ Inexpensive

More to see in the North and Northeast

ASKJA

If you want to get into the island's remote desert interior, then this is one of the places to head for. You can do it on a day's round trip from Reykjalíð, but the track is demanding and 4WD essential. Route F88 passes through a desolate landscape of gritty black lava and powdery yellow pumice, but it's worth it to see this vast caldera in the Dyngjufjöll mountains. It was formed in 1875 when the nearby volcano of Víti erupted, smothering much of eastern Iceland in ash. In the southeast corner of this massive natural depression is a smaller caldera, holding Öskjuvatn, at 217m (712ft) believed to be the deepest lake in the country.

Heading south on Route F88 towards Askja, you'll see a curiously symmetrical, black, flat-topped mountain looming ahead. This is Herðubreið, for centuries believed unclimbable because of its steep surrounding slopes of treacherous scree, until a German and an Icelander finally conquered it together in 1908. The greenery and vegetation here, fed by freshwater streams, come as something of a relief after all those barren miles of lava desert.

✚ 12E ✉ On Route F88; access strictly limited to Jul and Aug, be prepared for extreme weather conditions ❚❙ None ❓ Day tours from Reykjavík ☎ 464 1920; www.askjatours.is

BLÖNDUÓS

This settlement on Route 1 is scattered on the flat green land around the mouth of the River Blanda and is a good touring base. The town is unremarkable, but has a fascinating **Textile Museum** and a squat modern church of dark concrete, shaped like a volcanic crater and famous for its acoustics. There are salmon in the river and a rocky island called Hrútey, accessed by a bridge from the north bank, which is great for birdwatching. The Skagi peninsula stretches northwards, luring you on with a promise of good birdwatching and seal-spotting.

Don't miss the solitary stone-built church of Þingeyrar
(Thingeyrar) to the south of the town, which marks a wealthy
monastic site that was once central to the transcription of both the
Bible and the Sagas. It has a fascinating interior with a star-painted
ceiling and an unusual (English) altarpiece. Stand with your back to
it and you'll find figures watching you from the gallery.

🞧 7C ✉ 145km (90 miles) west of Akureyri 🍴 Various (£–££)
ℹ By the campsite ☎ 452 4520; www.northwest.is

Heimilisiðnaðarsafnið (Textile Museum)

✉ Árbraut 29 ☎ 452 4067; www.simnet.is/textile 🕓 Jun–Aug daily 10–5
✋ Inexpensive

BORGAFJÖRÐUR EYSTRI (BAKKAGERÐI)

For a town with two names, this is not a big place, but it is beautifully set on a broad bay, with a green valley behind and the dramatic mountain of Dyrfjöll (1,136m/3,726ft) beyond. There are good facilities for hiking and birdwatching in the area. With such a fine location, it's no surprise to know that the elves live around here in goodly numbers, notably inhabiting the small mound-with-a-view, Álfaborg. Look for semi-precious stones at your feet – you can see examples in the **Álfasteinn** museum and shop.

Iceland's famous landscape painter Jóhannes S Kjarval was raised near by at Geitavík, and you'll recognize the backdrop in his altarpiece in the church with Christ standing on Álfaborg.

www.borgafjordureystri.is

➕ 15D ✉ 336km (208 miles) east of Akureyri, on Route 94

Álfasteinn

☎ 470 2000; www.alfasteinn.is
🕓 Jun–Aug daily 10–6; Sep–May Mon–Fri 10–12, 1–5 ✋ Free

DALVÍK

Looking at this busy fishing town today there's nothing to show that it was almost destroyed by a massive earthquake in 1934. It's beautifully set near the mouth of Eyjafjörður, with mountains behind and a view of the large island of Hrísey across the water. It's worth the short ferry ride to enjoy the peace and quiet of the nature reserve here. Hrísey's other claim to fame is as a quarantine island for livestock and pets coming into Iceland.

The **Folk Museum** in Dalvík has displays dedicated to local giant Jóhann Pétursson, who grew to 2.34m (7.7ft) high and became a Hollywood film star. Behind the town you can explore the interesting wetlands of Svarfaðardalur; a good leaflet available locally lists the marsh plants here and details of several walks. To the north, the precipitous road leads on to Ólafsfjörður; the silver ship memorial overlooking the fjord is to a local boatbuilder, Eyvindur Jónsson, who died in 1746.

➕ 9C ✉ On Route 82, 44km (27 miles) north of Akureyri 🍽 Brekka Restaurant on Hrísey serves excellent Galloway beef, as well as lighter snacks ☎ 466 1751 ⛴ Scheduled ferry to Hrísey and Grímsey ☎ 695 5544 ❓ Whale-watching tours ☎ 863 2555; www.hvalaskodun.is

Byggðasafnið Hvoll (Folk Museum)

✉ Karlsrauðatorg ☎ 466 1497 🕐 Jun–Aug daily 11–6 and on request ✋ Inexpensive

GOÐAFOSS

Travelling along the road from Akureyri to Mývatn you'll see what looks like a cloud of smoke over to your right, as though someone were burning off the heather. This is spray from the mighty horseshoe falls of Goðafoss; you can park at the petrol station-cum-store at Fosshóll, cross the deep gorge of the River

Skjálfandafljót and follow the well-worn path to view this beautiful waterfall. It's called the 'falls of the gods' after an incident in AD1000, when the Lawspeaker at the Alþing (parliament) decided in favour of the country becoming Christian and duly threw all his pagan idols in the water on his way home. This is a good place to hunt for wild flowers in the heath – look out for the delicate white flowers of mountain avens.

✚ 11C ✉ Off Route 1 👋 Free 🍴 Coffee and snacks (£–££) at Fosshóll, also some accommodation ☎ 464 3108 🚌 All the tour buses stop here

GRÍMSEY

Contrary to popular expectation, most of Iceland lies south of the Arctic Circle, but this windswept island some 40km (25 miles) off shore is the exception, straddling the line at its northern tip. On a still, pink summer's evening, when the sun never quite sets on the horizon and the Arctic terns swoop overhead, it can seem a romantic spot, but the rest of the time there's not much to recommend it. The obligatory fingerpost which marks the circle line is a 25-minute walk up from the harbour, and offers the best photo opportunity. To the north the razorbills, puffins and kittiwakes that once formed an important part of the island's economy nest noisily on the cliffs.

➕ 10A ✉ 41km (25 miles) north of mainland 🍴 Veitingahúsið Krían, summer and weekends only (£–££) ☎ 467 3112 ⛴ Regular ferry from Dalvík, and excursion boat ☎ 458 8970 ✈ Flights from Akureyri with Air Iceland ☎ 460 7000

HÓLAR

Waymarked footpaths lead you around this attractive corner of the Haltadalur Valley. The first ever translation of the Bible in Icelandic was printed at Hólar in 1584. Until 1798 it was the seat of the northern bishopric, and the present cathedral is the fifth to be built here. It's worth a look in for the unusual chunky font of Greenland stone and the wonderfully vivid three-dimensional altarpiece, presented by Jón Arason, last Catholic bishop of Iceland, who served here from 1524 to 1550. After his execution at Skálholt (➤ 104–106) his body was brought here and buried under the separate belltower.

www.holar.is

➕ 9C ✉ On Route 767, 100km (62 miles) east of Blönduós ⊕ Church open daily 🍴 Summer snack bar in school building ♿ Free ❓ Guided tours of the church available 9–5 ℹ Old school building ☎ 455 6300

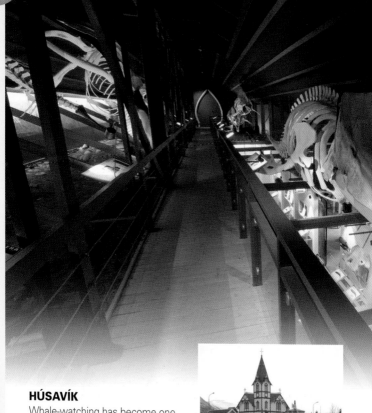

HÚSAVÍK

Whale-watching has become one of Iceland's most popular tourist activities and Húsavík, a pleasant fishing town on the western shore of the rolling Tjörnes peninsula, is deservedly its capital. Spotting success rates are higher here than anywhere else – you're more or less guaranteed a sighting of the small minke whales, and there's a good chance you'll see the nobbly snouts and classic tail-flukes of humpback whales here too.

If the conditions are right, you may even be lucky enough to spot fin, sei and killer whales (orcas). Take binoculars and sunglasses with you – the glare from the surface of the sea as you scour it for telltale puffs of whale-spout can be tiring. Don't miss a visit to the **Whale Museum** for a better understanding of these great sea creatures – there are whole skeletons to wonder at, a touch table (try the sharkskin!) and lots of fascinating information about the whales and dolphins found around Iceland.

Iceland's famous **Phallological Museum** is a collection of some 150 preserved animal penises and other items, relocated here from Reykjavík in 2005, and offers a different sort of exhibition for a wet afternoon.

➕ 11B ✉ On Route 85, 91km (56 miles) northeast of Akureyri 🍴 Choice of places (£–£££) 🚢 Whale-watching tours from traditional wooden fishing boats, may be combined with puffin-watching on Lundey island ☎ 464 7222; www.northsailing.is ❓ For an introduction to the high-tech world of fish processing, the Whale Museum can arrange a tour of the local freezing plant 🛈 Garðarsbraut ☎ 464 4300

Hvalamiðstöðin (Whale Museum)

✉ Hafnarstétt ☎ 464 2520; www.whalemuseum.is 🕐 Flexible opening daily, May and Sep 10–5; Jun–Aug 9–7 ✋ Moderate

Hið Íslenska Reðasafn (Phallological Museum)

✉ Hedinsbraut 3a ☎ 868 7966; www.phallus.is 🕐 Mid-May to mid-Sep daily 10–6 ✋ Inexpensive

from Husavík to Mývatn

a drive

Start from Husavík and take Route 85 north up the coast.

Enjoy the views west to the cake-shaped island of Lundey, teeming with puffins through summer, and even views of Grímsey on a clear day. After 4km (2.5 miles), the roadside monument is to poet Einar Benediktson.

Continue for 9km (6 miles) and turn into Hallbjarnastaðir to see the fossil museum. Retrace your route and after 3km (2 miles) turn right to Tjörneshöfn. The road to the harbour is steep and muddy – walk down if in doubt.

This is the best place to see the lines of compressed fossil shells in the cliffs.

Return to Húsavík, and stay on Route 85 towards Akureyri, crossing a big lava field covered with birch trees. After 39km (24 miles) turn left onto Route 845 for Laxárvirkjun.

This soon brings you to the pretty gabled farmhouse museum of Grenjaðarstaður; there's an ancient runic gravestone in the churchyard.

Return to Route 85 and turn left, to Laugar. At the junction with Route 1 turn left for Mývatn. Keep on Route 1 around the southern shore of the lake.

Lunch at the Hótel Gígur and stroll through green mounds scattered with periwinkles, or go on to Höfði for a picnic and walk through the birchwoods. Look out for whooper swans, tufted ducks, widgeon and Barrow's goldeneye on the lake, and listen for the drumming of snipe.

Continue to Reykjahlíð, and keep right on Route 1 for the sulphurous geothermal area of Námafjall, and Krafla power station 7km (4 miles) further on. Return to Reykjahlíð and bear right on Route 86 to return across the high moors to Húsavík.

Distance 195km (121 miles) **Time** All day, with stops for exploration

Start/end point Húsavík ✚ 11B

Lunch Hótel Gígur (££–£££) ✉ Skútustaðir near Reykjalíð

☎ 464 4455; www.keahotels.is

Fossil Museum ✉ Hallbjarnastaðir ☎ 464 1968 🕓 Jun–Aug 10–6

Grenjaðarstaður Folk Museum ☎ 464 3688; www.husmus.is

🕓 Jun–Aug daily 10–6

JÖKULSÁRGLJÚFUR

Best places to see, ➤ 42–43.

KJÖLUR

The high road through the interior known as Kjalvegur follows an old route between north and south, which has been used since earliest times. Kjölur is the bare valley at the mid-point sandwiched between the Langjökull and Hofsjökull glaciers. To the north, the road passes through high boggy country towards Blöndudalur; to the south the landscape is black and volcanic, stained with minerals and steaming areas of mud and sulphur. It feels cold here – there's a summer ski centre to the southeast on the flanks of Kerlingarfjöll. However, Kjölur holds a surprise – the geothermal oasis of Hveravellir, with hot springs of clear water, alpine flowers, a touring hut and campsite – and a weather station that is cut off from the world for most of the year. You can drive this route in a day in summer if the conditions are good; in winter it's for the off-roaders.

✚ 21H ✉ Route F35 runs between Gullfoss and Blöndudalur; www.hveravellir.is 🍴 None 🚌 Scheduled summer buses take this route daily between Reykjavík and Akureyri; www.sba.is

MÝVATN

Best places to see, ➤ 46–47.

SAURBÆR

The lovely sunny valley to the south of Akureyri is worth exploring for its four quite different churches, each found on a farm. You can loop up the west side of the valley on the 821 to Saurbær and return on